Financial Markets

Stocks, bonds, money markets; IPOS, auctions, trading (buying and selling), short selling, transaction costs, currencies; futures, options

Vol. 3

Thomas H. McInish, PhD

James Upson, PhD

DEDICATION

McInish: To Margaret McInish,

and Sheun and Ashley Aluko, with all my love

Upson: To my wife and children, with all my love.

TABLE OF CONTENTS

PREFACE

This book is written for market professionals and students who seek knowledge concerning financial markets. We focus on all four types of financial products: equities (stocks and warrants), debt instruments (bond and money market instruments), foreign exchange, and derivatives. We believe that in today's financial environment everyone must have a basic understanding of each of these markets. More and more individual investors are managing their own retirement portfolios. Both individuals and institutions are investing across borders so that it is not wise to only consider foreign exchange in international finance books and courses.

Volume 3 comprises 4 chapters that focus on understanding options, futures, and swaps. These are the major derivatives used by both speculators and hedgers. All business professionals need to understand derivatives. This is not just a topic for speculators or sophisticated professionals. As the population in developed countries around the world ages, they need to understand how to use derivatives to protect their portfolios and generate income.

Hedging is an important concept that all financial professionals and individual investors need to understand. We devote a chapter to this topic in Volume 3 because derivatives are the primary tools used in hedging.

Volume 1 comprises five chapters. Chapter 1 describes the ways that equities and debt are created, including initial public offerings, private placements, and auctions.

All financial assets have certain characteristics in common. All four product types are traded in markets, and, fortunately, the ways in which they are traded are limited. Chapter 2 describes the various trading venues such as exchanges and alternative trading systems and how trading is conducted such as in batch or call sessions and in continuous markets.

Chapter 3 explains the various types of transactions costs associated with trading financial assets. We cover both explicit transactions costs such as commissions and implicit transactions costs such as the cost resulting from needing to execute an order quickly. Chapter 4 discusses a topic that is frequently overlooked—clearing and settlement. Clearing and settlement involve the exchange of the financial assets and funds that result from trading. Historically, this topic has not been considered important for domestic investors. But as investors invest globally they encounter a wider variety of clearing and settlement practices. Also, the risks involved in clearing and settlement are greater in some markets than in others. Hence, the authors believe that understanding of this topic is essential for today's finance professionals and individual investors.

Chapter 5 deals with the regulation of financial markets. The particular institutions that regulate each market vary from country to country. But countries are increasingly coordinating their regulation of financial markets. During the crisis of 2008 governments worldwide cooperated in instituting bans of short selling. And efforts to combat money laundering and other financial crimes now have a worldwide scope.

Volume 2 focuses on understanding equities, debt, and foreign exchange. Chapter 1 describes the features of equities. Chapter 2 describes both the characteristics of debt instruments and the analysis of debt instruments, including the term structure, yield-to-maturity, total realized compound yield and duration. Chapter 3 describes foreign exchange markets. Foreign exchange has traditionally been neglected in studies of financial markets. Financial institutions have led the trend toward international investing. But recently the discount broker Charles Schwab introduced accounts that allow individual U.S. investors in trade securities in a dozen countries outside the U.S. in local currencies

Providing background for writing this book, the authors have traveled extensively, visiting exchanges, universities, brokerage firms, banks, and other businesses in many countries, including Argentina, Australia, Canada, Chile, China, Denmark, England, Finland, France, Germany, Greece, Hong Kong, Italy, Indonesia, Japan, Malaysia, Mexico, Lithuania, Luxembourg, the Netherlands, New Zealand, Norway, the Philippines, Poland, Portugal, Russia, Singapore, Spain, Sweden, Switzerland, Taiwan, Thailand, Turkey, Viet Nam and the USA.

CHAPTER ONE

FUTURES

Key Terms

Backwardation—spot prices exceed futures prices, or nearby futures prices exceed more distant futures prices.

Basis—the difference between the cash price of an asset and its futures price.

Basis risk—the possibility of incurring losses due to changes in basis.

Cash (also called Spot)—the market for more or less immediate delivery of an asset.

Cheapest to deliver—the concept that a futures contract price is determined by the price of the instrument whose cash market price and conversion factor make it the most economical to deliver.

Clearinghouse—an organization affiliated with a futures exchange that is the intermediary for all futures contracts and guarantees performance on all of the contracts.

Close out—to acquire an offsetting position.

Contango—authors disagree on the definition. According to some a market is in contango when the futures price is higher than the current spot price, which is the opposite of backwardation. Others state that a market is in contango when the current futures price is higher than the expected futures price, which is the opposite of normal backwardation.

Convenience yield—a return or benefit obtained from holding a physical asset.

Conversion factor—the relationship between the price of the contract grade specified as the benchmark grade for a futures contract and other deliverable grades.

Cost of carry—financing, storage, insurance and other costs of storing an asset for delivery in the future.

Cost of carry market—a market in which futures prices exceed spot prices by the cost of carry.

Delivery—the exchange of ownership of an asset under the terms established by the market on which the contract is traded.

First Position Day—the first day that a short is allowed to give an official notice of intent to deliver.

Initial margin—for a futures contract, the amount of cash or acceptable securities deposited at the initiation of the contract.

Long—the party that has bought a futures contract without acquiring an offsetting position and is obligated to take delivery of the underlying asset at maturity.

Maintenance margin—for futures contracts, the amount below which the margin in the account cannot decline without a margin call.

Margin call—a request for more margin.

Market-on-close—an order to be executed at the closing price or as near to the closing price as possible.

Maturity—the period within which delivery of the underlying asset can be made to satisfy the futures contract.

Net hedging hypothesis—the view that futures prices tend to rise (fall) over the life of a contract if hedgers are net short (long).

Normal backwardation—the view that the current futures prices is lower than the expected futures price so that futures prices tend to rise over the life of the contract.

Notional—a fictional amount used to represent the face value of the assets underlying the derivative contract.

Open interest—the total number of long (or short) contracts that exist at any given time.

Pit—the location on the floor of a futures exchange where treading occurs.

Position Day—the day on which the short first notifies the exchange of an intention to deliver, but not the first such day, which is called First Position Day.

Position limit—the maximum number of contracts that can be held long or short by a speculator.

Price limit—the maximum difference in trading price, either up or down, from the previous day's settlement price.

Quality option—the right to select what will be delivered on a futures contract.

Settlement price—the price established by an exchange for official use including the determination of the allowable trading range on the next trading day and the gains and losses to be posted to each account in the daily marking to market.

Short—the party that has sold a futures contract without acquiring an offsetting position and who is obligated to deliver the underlying asset at maturity.

Spot—see cash.

Spread (futures)—simultaneously shorting one futures contract and going long on another.

Timing option—the right to decide when to make delivery on a futures contract.

To arrive—a type of deferred delivery in which the price is based on delivery at a specified point and the seller pays the freight.

Variation margin call—a margin call in which the margin must be deposited with the same day and often within the hour.

Wild card option—for the CBOT Treasury bond futures contract, the right to announce an intention to deliver until 8 pm even though the settlement price, which is the 2 pm price, is fixed.

IN THIS CHAPTER, we explain how futures contracts work and provide additional information about the trading of these contracts. Specifically, we

- describe the origin of futures trading
- analyze each element of the definition of a futures contract to clarify its meaning
- describe the institutional arrangements involved in trading futures, including aspects of clearing and settlement such as clearinghouses, margin, marking-to-market, and settlement prices.

Then we discuss a number of features of futures market trading, including

- the profile of possible outcomes for futures contracts
- the relationship between cash and futures prices
- additional topics related to the economics of futures contracts such as the risks of speculative positions
- uses of futures contracts
- trading of futures contracts on stock indexes and individual stocks.

1. Introduction

Futures markets are used by hedgers, who seek to reduce or eliminate the risk they face from holding inventories, and by speculators, who assume the risk transferred from the hedgers. The primary economic role of futures trading is to allow those engaged in various lines of commerce to manage the risk they face due to fluctuations in the price of their inventory. These inventories comprise many disparate types of assets, including agricultural commodities, various precious metals, financial products of all types, and currencies. Inventory prices can fluctuate widely, and many businesses do not have sufficient capital to survive if the price changes are particularly severe. Historically, producers, consumers, and middlemen dealing in agricultural and mineral products have used futures. But today, futures on financial instruments dominate the market, and their growth is still continuing at a high rate.

Since the first introduction of contracts on financial instruments, volume has soared and the underlying assets have changed. In 1976, futures and options contracts traded on the Chicago Board of Trade (CBOT) comprised 128,568 contracts on financial instruments and 18,766,588 contracts were traded on agricultural products and metals. By contrast, in 2013 futures and options contracts traded on the Chicago Mercantile Exchange (which had merged with the CBOT) totaled 3.2 billion contracts of which agricultural commodities comprised just 14%.

2. How futures contracts work

2.1. A brief history of futures markets

From very early times, traders have entered into forward contracts for future delivery. Trading in **to arrive** contracts, a type of deferred delivery in which the price is based on delivery at a specified point and the seller pays the freight, began in Antwerp, Amsterdam, Breman, Le Havre, Alexandria, and Osaka from the seventeenth to the mid-nineteenth centuries. The first commodity exchange opened in Osaka, Japan, in about 1640 to trade actual rice. But the precursor of modern futures markets began with the trading of to arrive contracts in Chicago in the 1830s, before the development of railroads. In 1848, a group of 82 men founded the Chicago Board of Trade (CBOT), where both actual commodities and forward contracts were consummated. Gradually, the contracts became standardized with respect to the delivery period and grade, with allowances for price adjustments when the delivered grade differed. These developments caused more merchants to use the exchange and also led to the entry of speculators. Increases in the volume of trading led to decreased in the cost of trading, which, in turn, led to further increase in the volume of trading. Over time, the contracting process became more and more impersonal and more standardized.

But there were many instances in which members went bankrupt. In 1877, D.H. Lincoln, president of the Board of Trade (now the Chicago Board of Trade), was suspended and his accounts were settled for one-fourth of the amount due. In 1888, another president of the Board of Trade, Mr. Dow, failed and paid off his accounts at 40-50 percent of the amount due.

The records of the CBOT were destroyed by fire in 1871, but out-of town newspaper reports show that trading in modern futures contracts was already taking place in the 1860s. The introduction of the clearinghouse completed the process of developing modern futures contracts. The clearinghouse rigorously enforced margin requirements and spread the risk of loss due to failure over the whole membership, rather than just specific counterparties. Now, futures trading is conducted on exchanges around the world, including in Osaka, where the earlier contracts became the basis for futures trading. Today the Osaka Grain Exchange trades contracts in red beans and imported soybeans.[1]

The usefulness of futures trading is evident from its contribution to the economic development of Chicago. Grains from the US Midwest were sent to Chicago for use by that city and for transshipment to the eastern USA and throughout the world. A return flow of manufactured goods also went through Chicago. In the nineteenth century, the transportation system was poor. Roads were unpaved, so that rains often made them impassable, and there was a shortage of warehouse and dock facilities. Price of agricultural commodities fluctuated widely, often being very high just before harvest and very low just after harvest. The availability of futures trading contributed to the development of storage and transportation facilities, because business executives could build storage facilities and purchase grain with much less risk by locking in the sales price of the grain through the use of futures contracts.

In the 1970s, with the abandonment of fixed exchange rates under the Bretton Woods system, exchange rates began to fluctuate more widely. Interest rates also began to exhibit more volatility. These developments led to the introduction in Chicago of the first futures contracts on currencies and fixed-income instruments.

---

[1] Links to derivate-related web sites, including exchanges throughout the world, can be found at
http://www.slu.edu/departments/finance/638links.html.

2.2. The futures contract in detail

Futures contracts are traded on exchanges. Trades for nonmembers are made by **futures commission merchants**. Futures are standardized contracts in which one party agrees to sell (or in some cases to pay the liquidating value of the contract) to another party a specified amount of a product of a standardized quality at a specified future date at an agreed upon price. It is necessary to understand each element of this definition to understand futures. In the process of describing futures, it may be useful to consider specific contracts. In Table 1.1 we describe the basic characteristics the CME Group's US Treasury bond futures contract.

2.2.1. Standardized contracts in which one party agrees to sell to another party

All aspects of a futures contract are set in advance except one: the price. The price is determined on the floor of the exchange, or, for computer-based exchanges, in the exchange's computer.

There are two parties to a futures contract. The party that agrees to make delivery is called the **short**, and the party that agrees to take delivery is called the **long. Delivery** is the exchange of ownership of an asset under the terms established by the market on which the contract is trade. Delivery takes place in a predetermined and fixed sequence of events established by the exchange on which the contract is traded. It is common to use the terms **cash** or **spot** when referring to the market for immediate (within the normal settlement terms) delivery of an asset. Thus, when dealing with the US Treasury bond contract, a reference to cash would be a reference to a US Treasury bond available for delivery using normal spot settlement procedures. When dealing with currencies, cash trades are typically for 1- or 2-day delivery, in contrast to futures contracts, which initially call for delivery months in the future.

2.2.2. A specified amount of a product of a standardized quality

Each contract is for a specified amount of the asset covered by the contract. For an agricultural commodity such as wheat, the contract might

Table 1-1. Contract highlights for the CME Group U.S. Treasury Bond futures contract

Contract Size	One U.S. treasury bond with a face value of 100,000 USD
Deliverable Grade	U.S. Treasury bonds with remaining maturity of at least 15 years, but less than 25 years, from the first day of the delivery month. The invoice price equals the futures settlement price times a conversion factor, plus accrued interest. The conversion factor is the price of the delivered bond ($1 par value) to yield 6 percent.
Contract Months	The first three consecutive contracts in the March, June, September, and December quarterly cycle.
Price Quotation	Points ($1,000) and 1/32 of a point. For example, 134-16 represents 134 16/32. Par is on the basis of 100 points.
Tick Size	One thirty-second (1/32) of one point ($31.25), except for intermonth spreads,
Daily Price Limits	None
Position Limits	None
Last Trading Day	Seventh business day proceeding the last business day of the delivery month.
Delivery Method	Federal Reserve book-entry wire transfer
Last Delivery Day	Last business day of the delivery month.
Trading Hours (Globex)	SUN - FRI: 5:00 p.m. - 4:00 p.m.

Source: CME Group web site

call for the making and taking of delivery of 5,000 bushels. The CBOT US especially in connection with interest rate swaps, the face value or market value of the assets underlying the derivative is called the **notional** value.

The reference to quality derives from the fact that futures contracts originated for agricultural commodities. An agricultural contract might cover a particular grade of wheat. But the rules allow different grades to be delivered, and the futures exchange specifies how the price for one grade can be converted into the price for another grade. Thus, a conversion price for one grade can be converted into the price for another grade. Thus, a conversion formula, or **conversion factor**, indicates how to convert a price for the grade specified as the benchmark grade for a futures contract into a price for other deliverable grades.

For the US Treasury bond contract, quality has a closely related, but slightly different, meaning from that for agricultural contracts. The CBOT trades US Treasury bond contracts with a face value of 100,000 USD. In May, contracts for Treasury bonds trading on the CBOT had maturities in June, September, December, March of the next year, and beyond. Hypothetically, Treasury bond contracts could specify the exact bond that could be delivered on the March contract, on the June contract, and so forth. In other words, all the contracts might call for the delivery of a US Treasury bond with a coupon rate of 7.25 percent and maturing May 15, 2016. This approach has the advantage of simplicity. But there might be pro blames if the face value of the bonds contracted for through the futures markets was large in relation to the value of these bonds outstanding. Instead, a variety of bonds can be delivered on the contracts. Box 1.1 describes a related problem encountered in futures trading in Shanghai.

An alternative approach is to define what can be delivered in such a way that more than one US Treasury bond could be delivered. But this leads to a problem. Table 1.2 provides a partial list of US Treasury bonds that were eligible for delivery on the CBOT T-bone contract as of October 1997. The long value of the bond actually delivered. In the case of US Treasury bonds on the CBOT, the standard is that the bond cannot be callable or mature for at least 15 years, and the delivered bone is priced to yield 8 percent. The CBOT publishes conversion factors for each bond; showing how the price agreed to by the long and the short will be adjusted, depending on which bond was delivered. These conversion factors as of October 1997 also are provided in provided in Table 1.2.

Box 1.1. Shanghai woes

In May 1995 Chinese Treasury futures contracts, which were the most actively traded contracts on the Shanghai Securities Exchange in that year, were indefinitely suspended from trading. How did this happen?

Prior to their suspension, Chinese Treasury bonds traded at a premium over the bank deposit rate because of the government typically paid additional interest at maturity to compensate for inflation.

In July 1992, the government raised the bank deposit rate from 8.28 percent to 12.24 percent. Just before the bank deposit increase, bond 327 was issued with a coupon rate of 9.5 percent. The Shanghai Securities Exchange traded a futures contract with bond 327 as the underlying asset. The margin requirement was about 1 percent of the value of the underlying interest. Since Bond 327 was the last issue before the rate increase, there was a possibility that the government might unilaterally increase the yield on this issue by making a one-time payment at maturity.

One brokerage firm—Shanghai International Securities Company (Sisco), China's largest—did not believe that the government would make this adjustment. Another group of brokerage firms headed by China Economic Development Trust and Investment Corp., China's fifth largest brokerage firm, believed that the government would make this adjustment. These divergent beliefs set the stage for a trading war.

On February 23, 1995, the day the contract matured, trading exploded. During the last eight minutes of trading, contracts changed hands with a notional value of more than 28 billion USD, which represented more than three times the amount of Chinese government bonds issued during 1994. For the day, contracts with a notional value of more than 105 billion USD were traded. As a result of this trading, Sisco exceeded the 300,000-contract limit for members. Nonmember institutions were limited to 30,000 contracts, and individuals were limited to 10,000 contracts. Despite these trading limits, Sisco had placed one individual order to sell several

---

million contracts, but the exchange's computer did not detect this violation of the trading rules.

Just after the close of trading, the general manager of the Shanghai Securities Exchange and the head of the Shanghai Securities Administration required the head of Sisco to come to the exchange. Several hours later, they announced that all trades during the last eight minutes of trading were cancelled, but that other trades would settle on schedule. Following the close of trading, the government announced an additional coupon payment of 5.5 percent, which left Sisco with a substantial loss. But the loss was smaller than it would have been had the exchange not cancelled millions of contracts. Sisco was suspended, and an investigation was begun.

According to *Asiamoney*, "The exchange's announcement caused an uproar the following morning. Police lined the entrance to the exchange as a crowd of investors threatened to storm the trading floor," and the president of the exchange spend the next three days arbitrating disputes on settlement price.

(For additional information see *Shanghai Shanghaied* 1995.)

Since only one thing can be delivered on the JPY futures contract, namely spot JPY, quality is not an issue for this contract.

2.2.3. At a specified future date at an agreed upon price

Maturity is the period within which delivery of the underlying asset can be made under the terms of the futures contract. Some futures contracts are liquidated by a cash payment at maturity, so that there is no delivery. Also, some futures contracts have a single delivery day. But for most futures contracts, the short can initiate the delivery process at any time within a prescribed period. The delivery process can be better understood by examining a particular contract such as the CBOT contract for US Treasury bonds.

**Table 1-2. Conversion factors for selected bonds eligible for delivery
on the Chicago Board of Trade
10-year U.S. Treasury note futures contract as of 30 Oct. 1997.**

				Conversion factors	
		Date	**Issue**	**Dec.**	**Mar.**
Coupon	**Issue**	**Maturity**	**size†**	**1998**	**1999**
5 5/8	02/96	02/15/06	14.01	0.8746	0.8778
5 7/8	11/95	11/15/05	13.51	0.8907	0.8939
6 1/8	08/97	08/15/07	12.00	0.8859	0.8882
6 1/4	02/97	02/15/07	13.10	0.8980	0.9002
6 1/2	08/95	08/15/05	13.00	0.9251	---
6 1/2	10/96	10/15/06	10.00	0.9144	0.9166
6 5/8	05/97	05/15/07	13.95	0.9179	0.9199
6 7/8	05/96	05/15/06	14.00	0.9388	0.9406
7	07/96	07/15/06	10.01	0.9444	0.9456
7	08/96	07/15/06	10.00	0.9444	0.9456
Total Amount Eligible for Delivery:†				123.6	110.6

†Billion USD

Source: Chicago Board of Trade.

The delivery process on the US Treasury bond contract is a 3-day sequence. The short can initiate this sequence at any time beginning two business days prior to the first business day of the delivery month and ending two business days before the last business day of the delivery month. While deliveries continue through the last business day of the delivery month, trading for this contract stops on the seventh business day proceeding the last business day of the delivery month. As long as trading continues, the parties to a contract can close out the position by taking an opposite position. But once trading ends, the parties must make or take delivery.

There are a number of decisions in the hands of the short on a CBOT Treasury bond futures contract that may lead to profit opportunities. As we have indicated, the short side of a CBOT Treasury bond contract can choose from a variety of bonds to deliver. This right to select what will be delivered is called a **quality option**. Moreover, within limits, the short can decide when to deliver, which is called a **timing option**. For the CBOT Treasury bond futures contract, the short may announce an intention to deliver until 8 p.m., even though the settlement price, which is the 2 p.m. price, is fixed. This wild card option gives the short the possibility of making an additional profit if the price of a deliverable bond falls. Finally, after trading on the contract has ceased in the delivery month, the short can still pick one of several days as the delivery date. If the daily accrual of interest on the deliverable bonds is greater than the daily cost of carry, the short will choose to hold off on delivery as long as possible. Otherwise, the short will deliver as soon as possible.

The clearinghouse coordinates the delivery process and guarantees performance on the contracts, but does not actually make the deliveries, which are done by the parties themselves. The day on which the short first notifies the exchange of an intention to delivery is called the **position day**. The **first position day** is the first day that a short is allowed to give an official notice of intent to delivery. For the US Treasury bond contract, the first position day is two business days prior to the first business day of the delivery month, and this is the day the longs and shorts notify the clearinghouse of their open positions. On position day, the short notifies the clearinghouse that he or she intends to deliver, which initiates the delivery process. Once a delivery notice is filed with the clearinghouse, delivery cannot be cancelled. On the next day, called the "notice of intention day," the clearinghouse matches the oldest long with the delivery short, and the short invoices the long for the amount due for the sale. On the third day, the delivery day, the financial instrument is delivered to the long in exchange for the invoice amount. This completes the delivery process. There is no delivery of actual bond certificates. Instead, since US Treasury bonds are held in book-entry form only, they are transferred electronically.

The delivery process for the JPY contract on the SIMEX is less complicated, because there is only one delivery day and one financial instrument, JPY deposits, that can be delivered. Recall that for currencies, delivery is in the country of the currency being delivered at a bank designated by the clearinghouse, so in this case, delivery is in Japan.

2.3. Additional features of futures trading

2.3.1. Open interest

The number of contracts held long must equal the number of contracts held short at all times. In fact, the long and the short are just two sides of the same contract. The number of long contracts (or the number of short contracts) is called the **open interest**, so

Number of contracts long = number of contracts short = open interest

The open interest is the number of contracts actually in existence at any particular time. When trading in a particular maturity begins, there is no open interest. As market participants begin to place orders and trade with each other, the open interest grows. At any given time, exchanges trade a number of contracts that are identical except for their maturity date. The contract nearest to maturity typically has the largest open interest and the highest trading volume.

2.3.2. The clearinghouse

While the number of long and short contracts is equal in the aggregate, the individual contracts are not matched with each other until the maturity of the contract. In other words, the counterparty to a specific long contract is not a specific short, and the counterparty to a specific short contract is not a specific long. Instead, all longs and shorts are obligated to an intermediary, the **clearinghouse**. The clearinghouse guarantees performance on the contract among the clearing members, so the credit risk of the counterparties is reduced. After a trade on a futures exchange is cleared, the clearinghouse interposes itself between all clearing members. In the case of default, protection is provided by the customer's margin, by the equity of the futures commission merchant and clearing member, and finally by the reserve fund of the clearinghouse. In 1986, a large customer of Volume Investors, a clearing member of the COMEX, defaulted on a margin call. The clearinghouse seized Volume Investors' entire margin. Traders with accounts at Volume Investors lost their entire posted margin.

Because all contracts are standardized, it is possible to offset positions prior to maturity. If a long sells a contract (goes short), then the long and short positions are offset, and the clearinghouse cancels both positions, reducing the open interest by one contract. Shorts can also **close out** their position by acquiring an offsetting contract (i.e. by going long.)

Very few futures contracts for financial instruments are actually settled by delivery. Less than one percent of financial futures contracts on the CBOT result in delivery. Reasons for the infrequency of deliveries include:

1.   The cost of closing out a position is small, because commissions on futures contracts are typically round-trip commissions, so all of the commission is paid when the position is initiated, and there is no additional commission for acquiring and offsetting position.

2.   Exactly what can be delivered on a futures contract is specified in the contract and by the rules of the exchange on which the contract is traded. For many contracts, more than one item can be delivered. When the delivery is made (within the limits set by the exchange) is at the option of the party making the delivery – i.e., the short. Longs who have specific needs have an incentive to close out the position rather than accept delivery. In some cases, the long on a US Treasury bond futures contract may need bonds with a specific maturity or coupon rate. In this case, the long would not want to take delivery, since the short might deliver a bond that would not meet the long's needs.

3.   Location is not an issue in the delivery of financial assets. For nonfinancial contracts, there may be multiple delivery locations, in which case the short selects the delivery location. For these contracts, there is the risk that the delivery location selected by the short will not meet the needs of the long.

4.   For many futures contracts, the short can choose one of several days on which to make delivery. If a long wishes to purchase the securities on a specific day, then the position must be closed out and the purchase made in the cash market.

2.3.3. Open outcry

Historically, trading for futures contracts on many exchanges tool place through the open outcry system. In Chicago, trading takes place in the **pit**, a many-sided, staired depression where traders can stand to view and trade with each other. For active contracts, because of the large numbers of members who may be in the pit where the contract is traded, the open outcry method produces so much noise that is difficult to hear the bids and offers of potential counterparties. So the exchanges have devised a system of hand signals that are used along with the vocalizations (outcry).

In the open outcry method of trading, it is possible for trading to take place at different prices at the same time. One member may make an offer to sell at one price, and a second trader may make an offer to sell at a slightly higher price. A third trader may then simultaneously buy the contracts from both traders.

2.3.4. Settlement price

On stock exchanges, the closing price is the last trade of the day. But because futures exchanges are concerned that the last trade price may be stale, these exchanges determine a **settlement price** at the end of trading. This settlement price has a variety of official uses. It is the price that is used in determining the invoice price at the maturity of the contract. An additional use of the settlement price is in determining the daily transfer of cash between longs and shorts, described below.

2.3.5. Margin

To protect itself, the clearinghouse requires that each party to the contract deposit cash or acceptable securities such as US Treasury bills. This deposit is called **initial margin**. The economic function of margin for futures contracts differs from that for stock. For stock, margin is a form of down payment, but for futures, margin is a performance guarantee. Initial margin must usually be posted no later than the beginning of trading on the day after the trade day.

The amount of margin is typically based on the volatility of the asset that underlies the futures contract. Exchanges require more margin for assets that have greater volatility. In some cases, because the risk for hedgers is lower than that for speculators, the amount of margin is higher for speculators than it is for hedgers. Also, margin may be smaller for positions that involve a short position in one contract and a long position in another contract – i.e., a spread – if it is likely that there will be gains on one contract when there are losses on the other. An example is the SIMEX margin on the JPY contract when traded in combination with the SIMEX GBP contract.

Typically, the most difficult aspect of futures contracts to understand for people who have not dealt with them before is that the price negotiated does not change hands immediately. In fact, it is possible in theory, though extremely unlikely in practice, that no money will change hands between the long and the short prior to the maturity of the contract and the actual exchange of cash and assets. Futures contracts are marked to market daily. That is, each day the amount lost on losing contracts is transferred to the accounts holding contracts that have gains. The amount of gain or loss is determined by subtracting the settlement price for the previous trading day from today's settlement price and multiplying the difference by the number of units of the asset covered by the contract. This is different from most other markets, in which at least some cash changes hands among the counterparties shortly after the transaction is consummated. No money passes between the long and the short if the settlement price does not change from one day to the next.

At some point, if losses persist, the margin in the account will fall below the **maintenance margin** requirement, and the brokerage firm will ask the account owner to deposit more margin. The request for additional margin is called a **margin call**. Like the initial margin, the maintenance margin must usually be posted by the beginning of trading on the next day. If prices change substantially during the trading day, a clearinghouse may issue a **variation margin call**, a call for additional margin that must be posted within a short time, possibly within the hour.

With the growth of futures contracts on stocks and bonds, regulators have worried about coordinating the margin requirements for futures contracts and for the underlying assets. In the USA these concerns have led to a ban on futures contracts on individual stocks.

2.3.6. Daily price and position limits

Many futures contracts have daily **price limits** that prevent trading at a price that is higher or lower than a prescribed amount relative to the previous day's settlement price. If the equilibrium price moves outside this limit, then trading ceases and cannot resume as long as the equilibrium price remains outside the limit. On the next trading day, the new settlement price is the same as the previous day's price limit. Suppose that the US Treasury bond contract settlement price was 94 yesterday. Then, trading today cannot take place at prices outside the range 91-7. Suppose the equilibrium price moves to 99 and remains there for the remainder of the trading day. Then trading cannot take place. But the settlement price today will be 97, which is up the limit. Tomorrow the permissible price range will be 94-100, and if the equilibrium price is within this range, trading can resume.

There have been instances when the futures prices for agricultural contracts have been up or down the limit on a number of consecutive days. Therefore, no trading can take place. The exchange sometimes increases the limit to a level that allows trading to commence if it believes that this would be in the best interest of the market. The price limits prevent those in the market from experiencing margin calls that are too great on one day.

In some cases, exchanges limit the number of contracts that are permitted to be held net long or net short. The purpose of these **position limits** is to prevent one person or one firm from dominating the futures market or from being able to require the delivery of more of a particular asset than is readily available for delivery. These restrictions are more common on agricultural contracts than on financial contracts. The supplies of the latter are typically larger and somewhat expandable. Banks can create foreign exchange deposits, and there are active markets for lending stocks and bonds. But the supplies of agricultural products cannot be increased until the next harvest.

2.3.7. Accrued interest and invoice amount

In the USA bonds pay interest semiannually. A bond with a coupon rate of 6.5 percent and a face value of 100,000 USD pays 3,250 USD of interest every six months. When title to a bond changes hands between interest payment dates, the parties exchange the agreed-upon price plus interest accumulated for the number of days from the last interest payment date. This interest amount is called **accrued interest**. Interest accrues at the daily rate of (1/- number of days in half-year). The number of days in a half-year varies from 181 to 184, depending on the particular date and on whether the year is a leap year.

The conversion factor and the settlement price are used to determine the contract invoice amount at delivery as follows.

invoice amount = (contract size x settlement price x conversion factor) + accrued interest

The reason why the settlement price is used rather than the original contract price is that price changes between the original contract price and the current settlement price have already been compensated for through the daily mark to market.

3. The economics of futures contracts
3.1. Futures outcome profiles

Figure 1.1 shows the profiles of possible outcomes at maturity for futures contracts. (a) shows the long futures outcomes, (b) illustrates the short futures outcomes, and (c) presents both the long and the short positions on one graph. The value of the underlying asset is presented on the horizontal axis, and the monetary outcome is presented on the vertical axis. Short futures have the possibility of unlimited losses from a price increase. Even though prices are limited to falling to zero, such a decline will produce gains on a short futures contract so great that they are effectively unlimited. Therefore, we will sometimes refer to the gains as being unlimited, even though we know that this is not strictly true. Likewise, long futures positions can realize potentially unlimited gains from a price increase in the underlying asset, but losses are limited to the value of the contract at the initiation of the position. Because these potential losses are so large, we often view them as unlimited from a practical viewpoint, especially in relation to the initial margin.

3.2. The relationship between cash and futures prices

3.2.1. Cheapest to deliver

The short can deliver any asset that meets the terms established by the market on which the contract is traded. The traders in the market realize

Note: contract price = intersection of the lines with horizontal axis

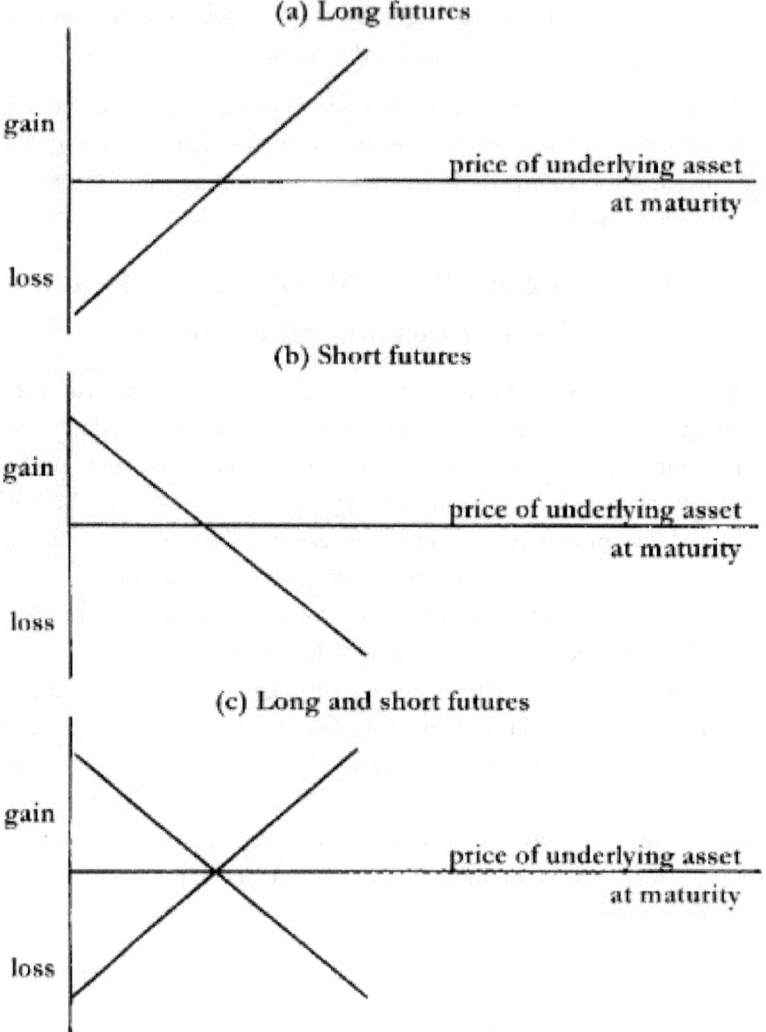

Figure 1.1 Profiles of futures contract outcomes at maturity

that the short will deliver the asset that is the cheapest to deliver, and the futures price reflects this fact. Consider three hypothetical bonds deliverable on the US Treasury bond contract that have the following conversion factors (CF) and cash market prices (CP):

Bond	CF	CP
#1	1.3620	1.3870
#2	1.1360	1.1360
#3	0.9760	0.9890

We ignore accrued interest. The implied cash price (ICP) is the price that is realized if an asset is delivered on a futures contract. For any given bond, its implied cash price (1CP) is

$$ICP = CF \times FP$$

where FP is the futures contract price. Assume that the futures price is 1,000 so that the invoice price for each bond per 1 USD of face value equals its conversion factor. The conversion factor, implied cash price, and cash price for each of these three bonds is:

Bond	CF	ICP	CP
#1	1.3620	1.3620	1.3870
#2	1.1360	1.1360	1.1360
#3	0.9760	0.9760	0.9890

Bond #1 will not be delivered, because its invoice price will be based on 1.3620, but its actual market value is 1.3870. Thence it would be better to sell this bond rather than deliver it on this contract. Likewise, Bond #3 will not be delivered, because its cash market price is higher than the price that would be received by delivering it. But Bond #2 will be delivered, because its cash market price exactly equals the price that will be received from its delivery.

The futures price is 1.0000 precisely because the implied cash price of Bond #2 is 1.1360. To see this, suppose that the implied cash price of Bond #2 increased slightly to 1.1370. At maturity, the short must deliver one of these three bonds. Suppose that a trader can go long this futures contract at 1.0000. Then, when Bond #3 is delivered, the invoice price will be based on the conversion factor of 1.1360, but the trader can immediately sell this bond in the cash market, and the proceeds will be based on 1.1370. Thus, going long this futures contract and selling this bond produces an immediate risk-free profit. Note that if we were not at maturity and could not immediately buy the bond and deliver it on the contract, the arbitrage profit must take into account the carrying costs of the bond and the interest costs of the daily marking to market between the time of purchase and the delivery date. But in either event, if an arbitrage opportunity exists, traders will buy futures contracts and/or sell Bond #3 in the cash market until the opportunity for a risk-free profit is eliminated.

Consider another way of looking at the concept of cheapest to deliver. Suppose that the US government repurchased all of Bond #2, so that it was not available for delivery. Then one of the two remaining bonds would have to be delivered. One possibility is that the futures price will increase to 1.013, which produces the following relationships:

Bond	CF	ICP	CP
#1	1.3620	1.3800	1.3870
#3	0.9760	0.9890	0.9890

In other words, the price of the futures contract has been bid up to 0.9890 (0.9760 x 1.0130) = 0.9890), so that the implied cash price equals the actual cash price, and Bond #3 is the cheapest to deliver. Due to arbitrage, this is the probable outcome. Alternatively, if the cash price of Bond #3 falls to 0.9760 instead, it is also economically feasible to deliver it on this contract when the futures price is 1.0000. Of course, it is possible for Bond #3 to become deliverable through a combination of an increase in the price of the futures contract and a decline in the price of Bond #3.

3.2.2. Cost of carry, contango and backwardation

Many assets that underlie futures contracts, including financial assets, can be bought and stored for future delivery. Costs associated with this storage include costs of the warehouse space, transportation costs, spoilage, insurance costs, and interest. Hence, if an underlying asset can be stored, the market would reflect **cost of carry**, and a **cost of carry market** is a market in which prices reflect the carrying costs. Because these costs accumulate over time, if future supply depends on the current rate of storage, then futures prices will be higher than current spot prices, reflecting the cost of carrying these items. In this case, the following relationship will hold.

$$F_{0,T} = S_0(1+r)$$

where $F_{0,T}$ is the price at time 0 for a futures contract maturing at time T, S_0 is the spot price of a commodity at time 0, and r is the cost of carrying the item from 0 to T expressed as a percentage of the value of S. In a full cost of carry market, the futures price equals the spot price times the quantity one plus the cost of carry. Otherwise, it will pay merchants to buy the product and store it future delivery. Some define a market in which futures prices are higher than current spot prices as **contango**. In March 1996, the prices of gold on the New York Mercantile Exchange for April, June, and August delivery were 399.60, 402.50, and 401.50 respectively. Figure 1.2 shows the time path of a commodity that reflects full costs of carry.

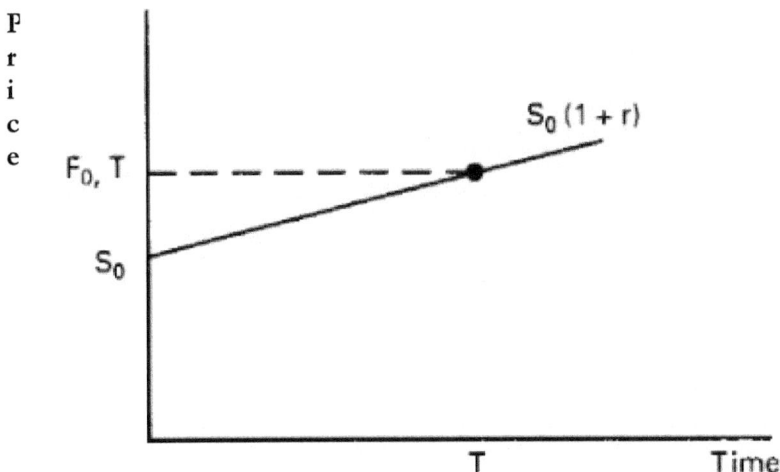

Figure 1.2 Full cost of carry

The concept of cost of carry applies to agricultural products, metals, and financial instruments. If the production of an agricultural commodity is seasonal, and the stock of the commodity is small relative to its rate of production, it is unlikely to be economical to store the commodity beyond a certain point. Suppose that a particular crop is harvested in May of each year. Within limits, the amount produced can be adjusted by adding more acreage to production, cultivating more intensively, and the like. In this case, it would not make sense to incur storage costs to hold the product beyond the next harvest. But the stocks of commodities such as gold and silver and of financial assets are large relative to the current consumption, so these are always being held in inventories. Box 1.2 shows the cost of carry calculation for the Value Line futures contract traded on the Kansas City Board of Trade.

The cost of carry, r, may not reflect full market rates for storage, interest, and other costs if some firms have cost advantages in these areas. Moreover, the cost of carry may be reduced. In some cases, holding

---

Box 1-2. Cost of carry for the Value Line futures contract

On March 26, 1999 the cash value line index closed at 892.08. Contracts on this index are traded on the Kansas City (US) Board of Trade (KCBT). Trading volume on these contracts is low and only the June contract traded on this day. Its settlement price was 891.20. What are the cost-of-carry values for this contract for the June, September, and December contracts?

The Treasury bill rates for the June, September and December contracts are, respectively: 4.46%, 4.60%, and 4.60%. The estimated yield on the Value Line Index is 2.0%. The closing value of the index (VLA) is and the number of days to maturity of each contact is: June, September, and December.

The cost of carry formula is

VLA*[1%+(T-bill rate - Value Line Investment Survey estimated median yield)]*
(Calendar days until futures expiration/360)
Substituting the June values gives :
891.20*[1%+(4.46 – 2%]*(81/360) = 694 basis points.

The cost of carry for the September contract is 1533 basis points and for the December contract is 2344 basis points. Note that the cost of carry values are increasing over time, reflecting a positive cost of carry.

Source: From the KCBT and its web site at http://www.kcbt.com/.

inventories provides firms with advantages, because they can use these in the manufacturing processes. It is possible that certain products are in short supply for current delivery, and that although the supply can be increased in the intermediate term, it cannot be increased immediately. Oil or grains may be in cargo ships headed toward our ports, but until the ships arrive, there may be a shortage. In this case, the physical asset is said to have a **convenience yield**, which may partially or completely offset the cost of carry. Moreover, any dividends or interest that can be earned must reduce the cost of carrying the financial instruments. Hence, the cost of carry model must be restated as follows:

$$F_{0,T} = S_0 (1+r-d)$$

where d is the convenience, dividend, or interest rate yield. If d>r, Figure 1.2 becomes Figure 1.3, and the market is said to be in **backwardation**. In March 1996, prices for live cattle on the Chicago Mercantile Exchange for delivery in April, June, and August were 64.55, 64.20 and 63.00 respectively. Hence, this market is in backwardation.

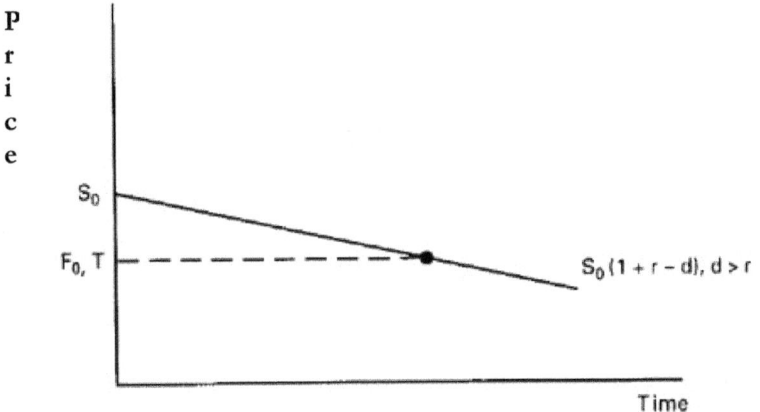

Figure 1.3 Backwardation

3.2.3. Basis

Basis is the difference between the cash price of an asset and its futures price. For agricultural commodities, basis can change because of changes in ability to deliver the underlying commodity at the designated delivery point.

A farmer growing wheat in Iowa may contract to sell that wheat in Chicago through a futures contract. But a shortage of transportation may cause prices to rise in Chicago and fall in Iowa. If the farmer cannot get his crop to Chicago, he will have to cover his short futures position at a loss and will also have to sell his crop in the cash market in Iowa for less. The possibility of incurring losses due to changes in basis is referred to as the **basis risk**.

At the maturity of a futures contract, the cash price at the delivery point and the futures price must be equal. Prior to maturity, basis may change daily even for contracts on financial instruments, although the causes are not always as obvious. Since financial instruments are delivery through the banking system, delivery costs are typically not an issue. But changes in interest rates can cause changes in the cost of carrying the securities, resulting in a change in basis. Changes in the instrument that is cheapest to deliver can also affect basis. Consider 24 bonds deliverable on the June 1990 US Treasury bond contract. Suppose than an investor held the bond that was cheapest to deliver. Naturally, the futures prices reflect the cash price of this cheapest-to-deliver bond. Next, suppose that one of the 23 other bonds becomes cheapest to deliver, so that the futures price now reflects the cash price of this bond. In this case, there has been a change in the basis for the cash bond that was originally cheapest to deliver.

3.3. Spreads

A spread involves simultaneously shorting one futures contract and going long another contract. This is done to take advantage of expected differential movements in the prices of the underlying assets. Futures spreads can involve two contracts for the same underlying asset on the same exchange but with different contract months, contracts for the same underlying asset but on different exchanges, or contracts for different underlying assets.

Suppose that a speculator believes that the British pound will weaken relative to the Japanese yen. Then the speculator can short a contract on GBP and go long a contract on JPY. If the expectation turns out to be correct, then both positions can be closed out, and the speculator will realize a profit if transaction costs are not too high. If a speculator expects the relationship between long and short interest rates to change, then a speculator can take opposite positions in a short- and long-maturity interest rate contract. Which contract is shorted and which is bought depends on the direction of the expected change in interest rates and which rate is expected to change the most.

A spread is typically less risky than taking an outright position. This is because in most cases, the prices of the underlying assets tend to move together. If interest rates rise, then both long and short rates tend to rise. The margin required on spreads is also typically less than on straight positions. But, of course, there are commissions on two contracts instead of one. In addition, the speculator must be concerned that both legs of the spread are put on simultaneously. On some exchanges, it is possible to enter both orders together and to specify the differential price that one requires if the order is to be filled.

3.4. Commissions

Brokers charge a commission for executing a futures trade for a customer. This commission covers not only execution services, but also accounting and other services related to a futures position. The commission may also cover costs of providing advice on trading strategies. Commissions may be fixed, or, as in the USA, negotiable. Only large customers have sufficient clout to actually negotiate commissions. When commissions are negotiable, there may be considerable variation in commission charges from firm to firm. Commissions may vary from contract to contract and may be lower for spreads than for long or short positions. Because positions that are not held overnight require less accounting and interactions with the clearinghouse, commissions for these trades may be lower.

In any event, the commission charges on futures contracts as a percentage of the value of the underlying asset covered by the contract are typically small. Their low cost, of course, encourages the use of futures in a variety of trading strategies.

3.5. A comparison of futures contracts and forward contracts

At this point, it may be useful to itemize some of the differences between forward and futures contracts.

Unlike forward contracts, the terms of futures contracts are standardized. Futures contracts are traded for specific delivery dates and amounts, and no deviations are possible. Forward contracts also have standard trading sizes and amounts, but it is possible to arrange customized terms.

The standardized feature of futures contracts, along with the use of clearinghouse as the counterparty to every contract, makes it possible to close out futures contracts prior to maturity without the knowledge or cooperation of a specific counterparty. The counterparty to a forward contract may not agree to close out the contract prior to maturity. In this case, instead of closing out the position, it is usually possible to arrange a second forward contract taking an opposite position with another counterparty. While this eliminates economic risk due to price fluctuations, credit risk is doubled, since there are now two contracts instead of one. Further, it will be necessary to make or take delivery on two contracts instead of one.

Futures contracts are marked to market daily, while there may be no transfers of funds between the counterparties to a forward contract until maturity. The marking-to-market feature of futures contracts reduces credit risk, but may make it more difficult to use futures contracts in the hedging transactions. Also, the marking-to-market feature of futures contracts causes the cash flow streams of futures and forward contracts to be different.

Many futures contracts have daily price limits, but there are no limits on the price movements of forward contracts.

Because of the differences between futures and forward contracts, especially the daily cash flows on futures contracts, the price for delivery on a futures contract will be different from the price for delivery on a forward contract if interest rates are stochastic—i.e., if interest rate changes are uncertain over time. Since we know that interest rates are stochastic, we expect futures and forward prices to differ.

3.6. Risks of speculative positions in futures

There are a number of ways of thinking about the hazard of taking speculative risks in futures contracts. It is widely believed that most futures traders (some say more than 90 percent) lose money. If we accept this 90 percent figure, then, since futures are a zero-sum game, the gain for the remaining 10 percent of traders equals the loss of the other traders less transactions costs.

What is the probability of losing all one's money in the futures markets? Examination of the gambler's ruin problem may provide some insights. Suppose that there are two players, the first with an initial stake of 100 USD; the second with a stake of 1000 USD. The players agree to toss a fair coin, with the first player paying the second 1 USD if the coin lands on side one; the second player paying the first 1 USD otherwise. The game will continue until one player is bankrupt. What are the odds that each player will be the one that goes bankrupt?

The probability of ruin for the first player is

$$1-(100/-1100) = 0.909$$

and the probability of ruin for the second player is

$$1-(1000/-1100) = 0.091.$$

Most small players who continue the game indefinitely are going to be wiped out. But this seems reasonable, since the rare small player who does not get wiped out is likely to be a big winner.

In assessing the risk of a futures position, one cannot simply look at the probability distribution of terminal futures prices. The reason for this is that any futures price that occurs prior to the maturity of the futures contract that is sufficient to exhaust the speculator's resources will bankrupt the speculator, so the position is closed out. In the case of a premature termination of the position, the ultimate futures price is immaterial.

From another perspective, in most markets all speculators are small relative to the market as a whole. Hence, large speculators may eventually go bankrupt even if they consistently take on only relatively small positions. And, of course, large speculators often take on large positions. Evidence for this viewpoint is seen in the occasional bankruptcy of large speculators. In

1979 and 1989, three brothers who were members of a wealthy Texas oil family accumulated very large positions in silver in both the cash and futures markets. As a result of their buying, the price of silver went from about 5 USD per ounce in 1978 to a price of almost 44 USD during 1980, but ended the year at about 16 USD per ounce (see Figure 1.4, which shows average yearly prices). At one point, the Hunts' profits were billions of USD. These large increases in prices greatly expanded the supply of silver as firms cut back on their use of the metal and reduced their inventories and as individuals melted family heirlooms to take advantage of the unprecedented prices. As a result, the price of silver began to fall.

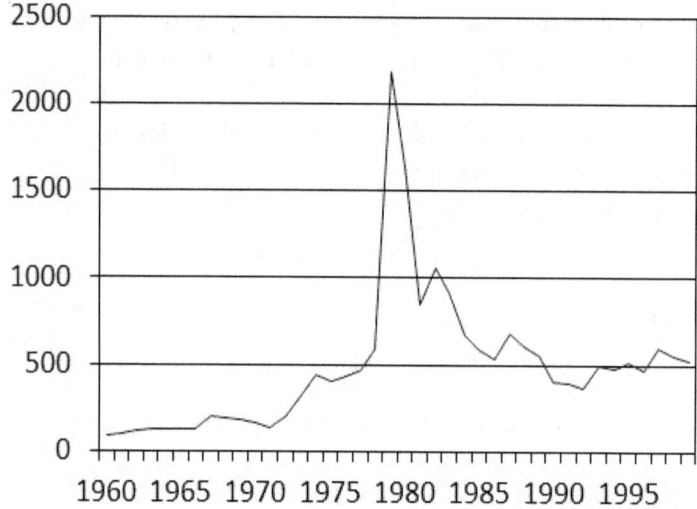

Figure 1-4. Silver prices monthly from 1960 to 1995

Eventually, the Hunts were faced with a margin call that they were unable to meet, which forced the liquidation of their futures positions. The Hunts lost not only their profits gained in the run-up on prices, but also lost most of their initial wealth.

3.7. Futures prices and expected spot prices

We have not yet considered the question: Is the current futures price an unbiased estimate of the future spot price? Obviously, for any particular futures contract, the futures price at any given time is unlikely to be the spot price actually realized. But over a large number of contracts, futures prices could accurately forecast future spot prices on average.[1]

The answer depends on at least two further questions: Are speculators risk-averse? Are futures contracts risky? We stated earlier that there are two reasons for taking positions in futures contracts: hedging and speculating. Hedgers are seeking to eliminate risk, while speculators are taking on the risk that the hedgers do not want. Why do speculators take on risk? If speculators are risk-averse, then they take on risk because the hedgers are compensating them for doing so. This is referred to as the **net hedging hypothesis**. In this case, if speculators are net long, then if they are to make a profit, the price of the futures contract must rise over the life of the contract. The theory that futures prices will rise over the life of the contract is called **normal backwardation**. If speculators are net short, futures prices are expected to fall over time, which is the opposite of normal backwardation. Some authors define this as contango, so that contango is the opposite of normal backwardation rather than the opposite of backwardation.[2] Figure 1.5 shows futures prices that represent normal backwardation and contango.

But if speculators were risk-neutral, they would not demand any compensation for bearing the risk that the hedgers transfer to them. In this case, we would expect futures prices to be unbiased forecasts of future spot prices. Or if speculators are risk-seeking on average, they might actually be willing to pay hedgers for providing the opportunity to take risks, just like the customers of a casino. Hieronymus (1978) and Gray (1963) argue that speculators are not risk-averse and that, consequently, futures markets provide hedging services at zero cost.

Even if speculators are risk-averse, futures prices might be unbiased estimates of future spot prices if futures contracts are not risky. At first, this

---

[1] According to Campbell R. Harvey's hypertextual finance glossary located at http://www.duke.edu/`charvey/Classes/wpg/glossary.htm , contango is "a market condition in which futures prices are higher in the distant delivery months," and backwardation is "the opposite of contango." Stoll and Whaley (1993) defines normal backwardation as "A market in which futures prices tend upward," and contango as "A market in which futures prices tend downward" (p.64). Also see
http://www.contingencyanalysis.com/glossary/backwardation.htm.

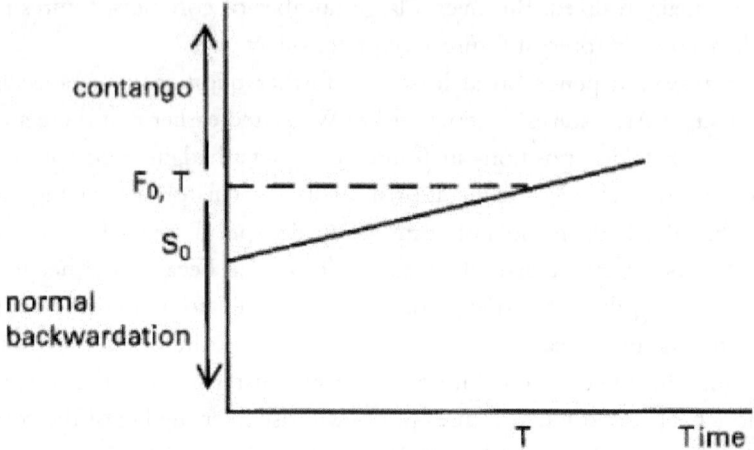

Figure 1.5 Net hedging hypothesis

might seem unlikely. But speculators, like all investors, should evaluate risk in terms of all their holdings. It is possible that futures contracts do not add to the risk of a portfolio, so that futures prices are an unbiased estimate of future spot prices.

4. Uses of futures contracts

4.1. The use of futures contracts in hedges

The principal use of futures contracts is hedging, and hedging activities provide the primary justification for the existence of futures markets. Futures contracts are not gambling, but instead permit increased production of goods and services by providing a way for producers, wholesalers and retailers to manage their risk.

4.2. Futures contracts as investment vehicles

Individuals and institutions can use futures contracts to expose their portfolios to fluctuations in the value of the underlying assets without actually owning those assets. They can provide an alternative to actually owning gold, silver, fixed-income securities, or stocks. We discuss futures on portfolios of stocks (stock index futures) below. The S&P 500 is a value-weighted index comprising 500 stocks, each in proportion to their total or aggregate market value. It would probably take some time to purchase each of the 500 stocks in the index. Further, a portfolio replicating the index might require may odd-lot positions or even fractional shares, which, of course, are not possible, not to mention bookkeeping and similar problems. A futures contract on the S&P 500 may provide the desired exposure while eliminating or minimizing many of these problems.

Some investors favor a strategy of holding a futures contract and at the same time holding a low-risk security such as a US Treasury bill with a face value equal to the value of the assets underlying the futures contract. In some cases, this strategy may provide a low-cost alternative to owning the underlying asset.

4.3. Using futures to manage the investment horizon

It is possible to use longer-term financial instruments and short futures positions to invest short-term or to use short-term financial instruments and long futures positions to invest long-term. Consider an investor in March who wishes to invest funds until June. There are myriad alternatives. One simple solution would be to buy a suitable government instrument such as a US Treasury bill with the appropriate maturity. Another alternative would be to buy a US government bond with a maturity of more than 15 years and to simultaneously short a US Treasury bond contract on the CBOT with a June maturity. The bond can be delivered on the contract in June. Thus, the investor has purchased a bond at a known price and has also locked in the sales price of the bond. Hence, the rate of return on this transaction can be computed (except for interest on the daily marking-to-market of the futures contract) and be compared with other alternatives for making short-term investments. At times the futures/spot strategy has produced higher returns than simply buying short-term instruments.

As indicated, it is also possible to invest long-term using a combined futures spot strategy. Suppose that one wanted to invest for more than 15 years. One possibility would be simply to purchase a bond with the e=desired maturity immediately. An alternative would be to go long a US Treasury bond contract with, say, a June maturity. In this case, the futures contract will lock in the purchase price of the bond that will be purchased in June. Then, one invests the funds from March until June using a short-term instrument. Of course, for this particular futures contract, one must worry about exactly what will be delivered. This may or may not be of primary importance, depending on one's investment needs.

5. Stock index futures, futures on individual stocks, and volatility futures

5.1. Stock index futures

There are a number of futures contracts traded on stock indexes. The S&P 500 Index traded on the CME is typical; Table 1.3 shows the basic features of this contract. At maturity, the value of the contract is 500 USD times the S&P Index value. There is no delivery of the underlying stocks, but instead the contract is settled in cash. The final settlement price is determined in a somewhat unusual way. Settlement prices are usually determined from prices at the end of the trading day. But by placing large **market-on-close** orders (orders to be executed at the closing price), large institutions can move prices temporarily and affect the closing S&P Index value. On the NYSE, where most of the S&P 500 stocks are traded, it is more difficult to manipulate the opening price than the closing price. The opening is a batch trade, and the value of trading at the opening price is typically the largest volume of the day. Moreover, if there is an imbalance of orders, the specialist can delay the opening and broadcast indicated opening prices in an effort to generate orders on the opposite side of the market. For these reasons, the CME switched from using the closing S&P Index value to the opening value in determining final settlement at contract maturity.

Specifically, for the S&P 500 Index contract, trading stops on a Thursday, normally the Thursday prior to the third Friday of the contract month. Then the settlement price for the expiration Friday is determined by the opening prices of the S&P Index stocks. If a particular stock does not trade

Table 1-3. Contract highlights for the ASX SPI 200™ Index futures contract

Contract Size	25 AUD per index point
Contract Months	March / June / September / December up to six quarter months ahead and the nearest two non-quarterly expiry months.
Tick Size	1 index point = 25 AUD
Daily Price Limits	None
Position Limits	None
Last trading day	All trading in expiring contracts ceases at 12.00pm on the third Thursday of the settlement month. Non-expiring contracts will continue to trade as per the stated trading hours
Trading hours	5.10pm-7.00am and 9.50am-4.30pm (For period from second Sunday in March to first Sunday in November); 5.10pm - 8.00am and 9.50am - 4.30pm (For period from first Sunday in November to second Sunday in March)
Settlement day	The first business day after expiry, ASX Clear (Futures) publishes the final settlement price of the contract. On the second business day after expiry, ASX Clear (Futures) settles cash flows as a result of the settlement price.
Cash settlement	There is no delivery. Instead all open positions at the close of the final trading day are settled in cash using the Special Opening Quotation of the underlying S&P/ASX 200 Index on the Last Trading Day. The Special Opening Quotation is calculated using the first traded price of each component stock in the S&P/ASX 200 Index on the Last Trading Day, irrespective of when those stocks first

trade in the ASX trading day. This means that the first traded price of each component stock may occur at any time between ASX market open and ASX market close (including the Closing Single Price Auction) on the Last Trading Day. Should any component stock not have traded by ASX market close on the Last Trading Day, the last traded price of that stock will be used to calculate the Special Opening Quotation.

Source: ASX website

on the expiration Friday, then its most recent trade price is used. This contract, like those of other index futures, is settled in cash, based on the closing value of the index, and there is no actual delivery of stock. Asian-style derivatives base the terminal settlement on an average of prices over a period of time. An example is the federal funds contract traded on the CBOT, which settles on the basis of the average daily federal funds rate during the expiration month (Chance and Rich 1996).

5.2. Futures on individual stocks

The San Paulo Stock Exchange and the Rio de Janeiro Stock Exchange traded forward contracts on individual shares beginning in the early 1970s. Subsequently, trading was begun in the 1970s in futures contracts on individual stocks (Braga 1996). Trading of futures on individual stocks began on the Swedish Futures and Options Exchange, OM Stockholm, and is now conducted there and on its sister exchange OMLX, the London Securities and Derivatives Exchange. The OM Exchange is a computer-based exchange. Both options and futures are traded on more than 20 underlying shares. The contracts typically cover 100 shares and are in one of three maturity cycles. A new six-month contract is listed every three months on the first trading day following the expiration of the near contract. Hence, there are always two futures contracts trading on each underlying security. The exchange has developed its own computer software for determining margin. Trading of futures contracts on individual stocks is also conducted on the Sydney Exchange and on OneChicago. The basic features for the OneChicago contracts are provided in Table 1.4.

Table 1-4. Highlights of OneChicago individual stock futures contract

Contract Size	100 shares of underlying security
Tick Size	$0.01 x 100 shares = $1.00
Trading Hours	8:30 a.m. – 3:00 p.m. Central Time
Position Limits	Apply only during the last five trading days prior to expiration: 13,500 or 22,500 net contracts, or Position Accountability (PA), as required by CFTC regulations.
Daily Price Limits	None
Reportable Position Level	200 Contracts
Contract Months	Any calendar month up to two calendar years (typically listing two front months and next two quarterlies).
Expiration Date / Last Trading Day	For monthly contracts, the third Friday of contract month or, if such Friday is not a business day, the immediately preceding business day. Expiry is at the close of the trading day. For weekly contracts, the day of the week indicated by the ticker symbol and expiration date. Expiry is at the close of the trading day.
Settlement/Delivery	For monthly contracts, physical delivery of underlying security on third business day following the Expiration Day. For weekly contracts, physical delivery of

	underlying security on first business day following the Expiration Day.
Margin Requirements	Minimum initial and maintenance margin requirement of 20% of the cash value of the contract. Certain offsets may apply
Short Sale	No Reg SHO requirements
Clearing and Settlement	Trades executed at OneChicago are cleared and settled by OCC, formally known as The Options Clearing Corporation.

Source: OneChicago website

5.3. Volatility of futures

OMLX, the London Securities and Derivatives Exchange, trades a number of futures contracts which fluctuate in value based on changes in the volatility of an underlying asset. The underlying assets whose volatility is tracked include the German DAZ stock index, the Swedish OMX index, and the British FTSE 100. There are no position limits on these contracts.[1]

6. Summary

"To arrive" contracts were traded before the 1900s in Antwerp, Amsterdam Bremen, Chicago, Le Havre, Alexandria and Osaka. Modern futures contracts evolved in Chicago during the late 1800s. The two most important developments were standardization and impersonalization. Standardization simplifies trading, since only the price must be negotiated. Impersonalization makes it possible to close out contract positions prior to maturity by reversing the initial trade. Impersonalization also eliminates the need to assess the credit of a particular counterparty by substituting a clearinghouse as the counterparty for all contracts. The clearinghouse guarantees performance among the clearing members on all contracts and

---

[1] Additional information is available at
http://www.crbindex.com/conspecs/omlx/iindex.htm.

manages a system of margins, or performance payments. Most people are used to thinking about spot or cash markets, where prices for the more or less immediate delivery of assets are negotiated. In futures markets, the prices negotiated are not for immediate delivery, but, instead are for delivery at a date that may be months in the future.

There are two parties to a futures contract, the long, who agrees to take delivery, and the short, who agrees to make delivery. The value of the contracts is marked-to-market daily. The exchange posts a settlement or official price that is used in determining gains and losses. If margin falls below the maintenance margin requirement a margin call requiring additional margin is issued. For some contracts, only prices that are within a specified range around the previous day's settlement price are permitted. The number of contracts that an individual or group acting together can own may also be limited.

Some futures contracts permit more than one asset to be delivered and some also permit delivery over a number of days at the end of the contract. Within exchange rules, the choice of what is delivered and when it is delivered is the prerogative of the short. Because shorts deliver the asset that is most economical, based on a comparison of futures and cash prices, the futures price is determined by the price of the asset that is cheapest to deliver. Some traders and speculators undertake positions known as spreads by simultaneously going long one contract and shorting another contract to take advantage of expected changes in the relative prices of the two contracts.

When futures prices are above the current cash prices, the market is in contango, and when futures prices are below the current cash prices, the market is in normal backwardation. Contango can result from a market that primarily reflects storage costs, while normal backwardation may reflect high current demand when supplies cannot be increased in the short term. If speculators are risk-adverse, contango and normal backwardation can reflect the need to attract long or short speculators to bear the risk transferred from hedgers.

The difference between the cash price for an asset and the futures price is called "basis." Basis, which can change from trade to trade, affects the cash flows of the contract and also the effectiveness of the contract in hedging.

Questions

1. What is the definition of a futures contract?

2. What is the meaning of the term "notional?"

3. How does a conversion factor play a role in a futures contract?

4. What is the role of the clearinghouse?

5. How does initial margin differ from maintenance margin?

6. How does margin for futures differ from margin for equities?

7. Explain the concept of "cheapest to deliver."

8. What is the difference between contango and normal backwardation?

9. What are the similarities and differences between forward and futures contracts?

10. What is the principal use of futures contracts?

References

Braga, Bruno Saturnino 1996: Derivatives markets in Brazil: An overview. *Journal of Derivatives* 4, 63-78.

Chance, Don M. and Rich, Don R. 1996: Asset swaps with Asian-style payoffs. *Journal of Derivatives* 3, 64-77.

Gray, Roger 1963: Onions revisited. *Journal of Farm Economics* 45; repr. In *Selected Writings on Futures Markets*, vol 2., ed. A.E. Deck (Chicago: Chicago Board of Trade, 1997), 325.8.

Hieronymus, Thomas A. 1978: *Economics of Futures Trading*. New York: Commodity Research Bureau. *Shanghai Shanghaied* 1995, *Asiamoney* 6 (Oct.), 15-20.

Stoll, Hans R. and Whaley, Robert E. 1993: *Futures and Options: theory and application*. Cincinnati, OH: South-Western.

CHAPTER TWO

OPTIONS

Key Terms

American option—an option that can be exercised at any time prior to expiration.

At the money—the price of the underlying asset equals the striking price.

Bear spread—a spread that is profitable when the price of the underlying asset decreases.

Bull spread—a spread that is profitable when the price of the underlying asset increases.

Calendar spread—the purchase of one option and the sale of another, both with the same striking price, but with different expiration dates.

Call—an option that gives the owner the right, but not the obligation, to buy an underlying asset at a fixed price, or in some cases to receive the liquidating value in cash.

Covered—writing an option while owning an offsetting position in the underlying asset or its equivalent.

Delta—the change in the price of an option in response to a change in the value of the underlying asset.

European option—an option that can be exercised only at expiration.

Excess premium—the difference between the premium of an option and its minimum value.

Exercise price—see striking price.

Expiration date—the date on which the option contract terminates.

Gamma—the change in an option's delta in response to a change in the price of the underlying asset.

In the money—for a call, the price of the underlying asset is greater than the striking price; for a put, the price of the underlying asset is less than the striking price.

Intrinsic value—same as minimum value.

Implied volatility—an estimate of an asset's volatility that is obtained from the options market.

Leg—one of the two transactions of a spread or straddle.

Minimum value of an option—ignoring interest, the greater of (1) the amount the option is in the money, or (2) zero.

Moneyness—a collective reference to in the money, at the money, and out of the money.

Naked—writing an option without owning an offsetting position in the underlying asset or its equivalent.

Neutral spread—a spread that is profitable when the price of the underlying asset is unchanged.

Open interest—the number of contracts that are currently in existence which is the sum of the number of contract owned and the number of contracts written divided by 2.

Option Clearing Corporation—an organization that clears and becomes the counterparty of all exchange-traded option contracts in the U.S.

Out of the money—for a call, the price of the underlying asset is less than the striking price; for a put, the price of underlying asset is greater than the striking price.

Premium—the price of an option contract.

Price spread—the purchase of one option and the sale of another, both with the same maturity, but with different striking prices.

Put—an option that gives the owner the right, but not the obligation, to sell an underlying asset at a fixed price, or in some cases to receive the liquidating value in cash.

Put-call parity—for European options, the sum of the put premium and the price of the underlying asset must equal the sum of the call premium plus the present value of the exercise price.

Rho—the rate of change of the value of the option with respect to interest rates.

Spread—the simultaneous purchase of one option contract and the sale of another.

Straddle—the purchase or sale of both a put and call on the same stock.

Striking price—the price at which the exchange of the underlying asset, or its equivalent in cash, will take place.

Time spread—see calendar spread.

Time value—see excess premium.

Theta—the rate of change in the value of an option related to the change in the length of time until its expiration.

Uncovered—see naked.

Vega—the change in an option's value with respect to a change in the volatility of the underlying asset.

Volatility spread—see straddle.

Writer—the party that has sold an option contract other than in a closing transaction.

THIS CHAPTER describes options contracts. Specifically, we
- Introduce a number of basic terms used in options markets
- Describe over-the-counter and exchange-traded options
- Describe options premiums and related concepts
- Describe how options are exercised

Then, we
- Review reasons for using options
- Explain the risks of using options
- Introduce several options trading strategies
- Provide detailed information concerning actual options on individual stocks, futures contracts, and indexes.

1. Introduction

Options were traded over-the-counter in the U.S. until 1973 when the Chicago Board Options Exchange (CBOE) began trading option contracts. These exchange-traded contracts are standardized so that only the price paid by the buyer to the seller is determined on the exchange. Trading in options has grown steadily and during the year ended December 2013 more than 1.1 billion option contracts were traded on the CBOE.[1] Options are now traded on ten additional exchanges in the USA and on many exchanges throughout the world.[2]

Initially, exchange-traded options were contracts for the purchase or sale of common stock of particular companies. The types of financial assets covered by exchanged traded options have been broadened to include indexes and futures contracts. Stock indexes were the first to be covered by option contracts, but options now cover a diverse array of financial products, including indexes measuring losses from natural catastrophes such as earthquakes.

This chapter describes option contracts. In section 2, we present basic terms that are needed to understand option markets. Then we describe the way trading in option contracts is done both over-the-counter and on exchanges. Next, we explore the pricing of option contracts. Then we describe the process of exercising options and the circumstances under which they are likely to be exercised.

In the second part of this chapter, we describe why investors buy and sell options and the risks of trading options. We also explain several common options trading strategies used by investors and describe representative options on individual equities, futures contracts, and indexes.

---

[1]

http://www.cboe.com/AboutCBOE/AnnualReportArchive/AnnualRepor t2012.pdf

[2] http://www.sec.gov/answers/options.htm

2. How options work

2.1. Option terminology

An option is a contract in which one party gives another party the right, but not the obligation, to buy or sell an underlying asset (which is sometimes called an underlying interest), or its value in monetary terms, at a stated price. The party that grants the right is called the writer and the party that receives the right is called the owner. The price at which the owner of the contract and the writer exchange the underlying asset is called the strike price or the exercise price. If the option is a put option, upon exercise the owner delivers the underlying asset (or its value in cash) to the writer. If the option is a call option, upon exercise the writer delivers the underlying asset (of its value in cash) to the owner.

Both American and European style options are traded in the U.S. and Europe as well as around the world. European style options can only be exercised at maturity. American style options can be exercised at any time during their life until the option expiration. For European options, the expiration date is the day on which the option can be exercised, while for American options it is the last day the option can be exercised. The origin of the terms European and American in referring to options is not known. Because the right to exercise at more times has value, an American option is typically slightly more valuable than a European option.

When the writer and owner enter into an option contract, the owner pays the writer a sum of money, which is called the option **premium**. The margin on the purchase of an option contract is 100%, so that the buyer must pay the entire premium by settlement day. Settlement of option contracts in many option markets is on day t+1, compared to stock market settlement on day t+3. The owner must have sufficient cash or, if the owner has a margin account, sufficient buying power.

If the writer of a call option owns the underlying asset, the writer is **covered**. Covered writers may have a position in the actual underlying asset or in another option. As a specific example, if a trader writes a call for 100 shares of stock BC and also owns 100 shares of stock BC, then the trader is a covered call writer. If the writer of a put has a short position in the underlying asset, the writer is covered. Specifically if a trader writes a put contract for 100 shares of BC and then short sells 100 shares of BC, the writer of the put is covered. If the writer of an option does not have an offsetting position in the underlying asset, then the position is **naked** or **uncovered**. There may be no margin required for covered writing and the writer may even be able to spend the premium. The margin required for naked writing is generally a percentage of the value of the underlying asset. If the equity in an option writer's account falls below the maintenance margin requirement, the writer receives a margin call, a request for additional margin. Because of the short settlement time and the volatility of option values, many firms will not allow customers to buy or write options unless the money is already in the customer's account.

For European options with the same maturity and striking price, there is a special relationship between put and call prices called put-call parity. Put-call parity is valid for any asset type with a European option. Let P = the put premium, C = the call premium, X = the exercise price, S = the current price of one unit of the stock, r = the risk free interest rate until the exercise date, and T be the time in years until the exercise date. Then

$$P + S = C + e^{-rT} X \tag{1}$$

In words, the value of a put option plus one share of stock is equal to the value of a call option plus cash equal to the present value of the strike price of the option. The put call parity relationship can be used to change the form of a transaction, which may be advantageous if laws limit some kinds of trading practices.

Short selling is banned in some countries; although several of these countries have option markets that trade in tandem with the stock markets. Synthetic short positions in a stock can be created using put-call parity. Rearranging equation (1) we arrive at

$$-S = P - C - e^{-rT} X \tag{2}$$

The -S indicates the sale of the stock. In words, equation (2) states that a short sale of stock is equivalent to buying a put, writing (selling) a call, and lending the present value of the strike price of the option at the risk free rate. Note that from a cash flow perspective lending money is the same as purchasing a bond. Even when securities laws allow for short selling, synthetic short sales are often used for two primary reasons. First, to conduct a short sale, the short seller must be able to borrow the stock. Sometimes however, there is no stock that is available to borrow, forcing the trader to use a synthetic short. Second, borrowing stock is not free. When the costs of borrowing stock are high, traders may turn to synthetic short sales in order to avoid these high borrowing costs.[1]

A call is **in the money** if the price of the underlying asset is greater than the striking price. A put is in the money if the price of the underlying asset is less than the striking price. A call is **out of the money** if the price of the underlying asset is less than the striking price and a put is out of the money if the price of the underlying asset is higher than the striking price. When the price of the underlying asset equals the striking price both puts and calls are **at the money**. At maturity if the call is in the money, the call will have the value $S - X$ and the put will have no value. At maturity, if the put is in the money, the call will have no value and the put will have the value $X - S$. If the option is at the money at maturity, $X = S$ and both the put and call have no value. Collective references to whether an option is in the money, at the money, or out of the money is called **moneyness**.

2.2. Over-the-counter options

For many years and continuing today, options have been traded in the over-the-counter market. In this market those seeking to enter into option contracts approach an option dealer, possibly through a regular brokerage firm. The terms of the contract are negotiated and the deal is struck. When the deal is consummated the owner pays a fee to the writer. Because it is the inducement for the writer to enter into the risky contract, the fee is called the premium, just like the payment that a policyholder makes to an insurance company in compensation for issuing a policy.

The dealer can either act as the counterparty or find another party willing to be the counterparty. Investment bankers have sophisticated departments willing to write various kinds of options. But these are typically available only in large sizes. These banks do not attempt to manage their risk

---

[1] Knoll (1994). The sale of assets combined with the use of option contracts was used in the Middle Ages in Europe to avoid prohibitions against the charging of interest.

resulting from being the counterparty to all of these contracts on a contract-by-contract basis. Instead, they manage the risk of their entire derivative portfolio.

The Chicago Board Options Exchange competes with the over-the-counter options market by allowing for more flexibility in exchange-traded options. In 1993 the Chicago Board Options Exchange began trading FLexible EXchange (FLEX) options, which permit institutional traders to negotiate strike prices over a wide range rather than simply trading the exchange's pre-specified contracts. FLEX contracts require a minimum notional principle of $10,000,000. In early 2013 daily volume exceeded 15 million contracts. A key advantage of FLEX options compared to over-the-counter options is that the FLEX option is guaranteed by the Option Clearing Corporation. This virtually eliminates counterparty risk, the risk that the counterparty to the option contract will not fulfill the terms of the contract.[1]

2.3. Exchange-traded options

In the early 1970s, exchanges began developing and trading options contracts. Some older established exchanges such as the Philadelphia Stock Exchange began to trade options and in some cases separate exchanges such as the Chicago Board Options Exchange (CBOE) have been established to trade options.

Exchange-traded options are made possible by the standardization of contracts. Each contract specifies the (1) underlying interest, (2) striking price, and (3) expiration date. The only thing negotiated on the exchange is the option price, which is still called the premium.[2] Unlike over-the-counter options, exchange-traded options are depersonalized in that the writer and the owner are not paired until the owner decides to exercise. Instead, all contracts are with an intermediary. In the U.S. this intermediary is the Option Clearing Corporation, an entity organized by the exchanges for the purpose of serving as the counterparty for all options contracts. Since a

---

[1] http://www.marketswiki.com/mwiki/CBOE_FLEX_options

[2] As we discuss below, this means that the term premium means something different for options and for warrants even though warrants are similar to options.

specific individual or firm is not a counterparty, traders do not have to worry about the ability of the counterparty to perform on the contract. Because all contracts are identical, it is possible to enter into an option contract and, subsequently, close out the position prior to expiration by acquiring an offsetting position. To close out a position, a writer buys a contract and an owner sells a contract. The number of options written is equal to the number of options owned. The open interest is the number of contracts that are currently in existence, i.e., number of contracts owned = number of contracts written = open interest.

Option markets, just like the markets for equities, futures, and foreign exchange, now are dominated by electronic exchanges. Electronic exchanges have reduced the costs of trading, increased the speed of trading, and simplified the option trading process.[1] The Chicago Board Options Exchange adopted complete electronic markets in 2003. The electronic trading of options is one reason that option contract volume has surged in recent years. Electronic trading also allows for better price integration between option and stock markets. Recall from the put-call parity equation that the price of a put and call are directly linked. If, for example, the price of a stock increases by one penny (0.01 USD), then, ceteris paribus, the value of every put and call on the stock will also change. An actively traded stock may have 20 put and call option contracts available in each month for the next 24 months. The one penny price change in the stock will then create price changes on 20 x 24 = 480 option contracts. In addition, for actively traded stocks, there can be many one penny price changes for every second of trading.

Just as the markets for equities, futures, and foreign exchange trading have become dominated by electronic exchanges, so have the option markets. Electronic exchanges have reduced the costs of trading, increased the speed of trading, and simplified the option trading process. The Chicago Board Option Exchange became a completely electronic market in 2003. The electronic trading of options is one reason that option contract volume has surged over recent years. Electronic trading also allows for better price

---

[1]

http://www.businessweek.com/magazine/content/05_22/b3935117_mz0 20.htm integration between option and stock markets. Recall from the put-call parity equation that the price of a put and call are directly linked to the current price of a stock or other underlying asset. If, for example, the price of a stock increases by one penny (0.01), then the value of every put and call on the stock will also change. An actively traded stock may have 20 put and call option contracts available in each month for the next 24 months. The one penny price change in the stock will then create price changes on 20 x 24 = 480 option contracts. In addition, for actively traded stocks, there can be many one penny price changes for every second of trading.

2.4. The option premium and related concepts

2.4.1. The minimum value of an option

We have seen that the writer and owner exchange the option premium at the initiation of the option contract. Whether or not to exercise is at the discretion of the owner. The owner will not exercise the option if exercising will reduce the owner's wealth. Hence, the minimum value of an out of the money or at the money option must be zero.

Let X = the strike price, Pu = the price of the underlying asset, and Xp = the present value of X. The minimum value of an American style put is max $(0, X - S)$ and the minimum value of an American style call on a dividend paying stock is max $(0, S - X)$. The owner of a European style put can lock in the difference between the current value of the underlying asset, S, and the present value of the exercise price, Xp. Hence, the minimum value of the European style put is max $(0, Xp - S)$. Likewise, the owner of an American style call on a non-dividend paying stock can lock in the difference between S and Xp or $S - Xp$. The maximum value of this option is max $(0, S - Xp)$. Since each writer is the counterparty to an owner, the value of the writer's position is decreasing when the value of the corresponding owner is increasing.

In summary, assuming an interest rate of 0%, the **minimum value of an option** is the greater of (1) the amount the option is in the money, or (2) zero. The minimum value is sometimes called the intrinsic value.

Figure 2-1 illustrates the changes in the value of an ownership interest in an asset as the prices of the asset changes. An increase in the price increases the value of a long position and decreases the value of a short position. A decrease in the price decreases the value of a long position and increases the value of a short position.

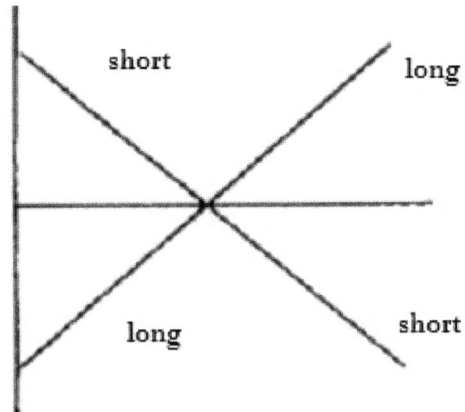

Figure 2.1. Profiles of long and short positions

Let Pi, the initial price of an asset, be the point of intersection of the two straight lines in Figure 2-1 and Pu be the current price of the asset. For a long position, the value of the ownership interest is Pu = Pi, which increases when Pu increases. For a shot position, the change in the value of the ownership interest Pi – Pu, which increases when Pu decreases.

Options are contracts that give the owner the right to buy (call) or sell (put) an asset at a specified price. Assume that the specified price is X. Then the two lines illustrated in Figure 2-1 can be transformed to illustrate the minimum values of four possible option contracts with a contract with X as the exercise price: Quadrant 1, long call; quadrant 2, long put; quadrant 3, short put; quadrant IV, short call. These four possibilities are presented in Figure 2-2. Note that buying a call and writing a put are equivalent (in economic terms) to owning and asset and buying a put and writing a call are equivalent (in economic terms) to shorting an asset.

Note that these payoffs illustrated in Figure 2-2 assume that the premium on the options is zero. If the premiums are not zero, at maturity, the owners' outcomes are reduced by the amount of the premium and the writers' outcomes are increased by the amount of the premiums.

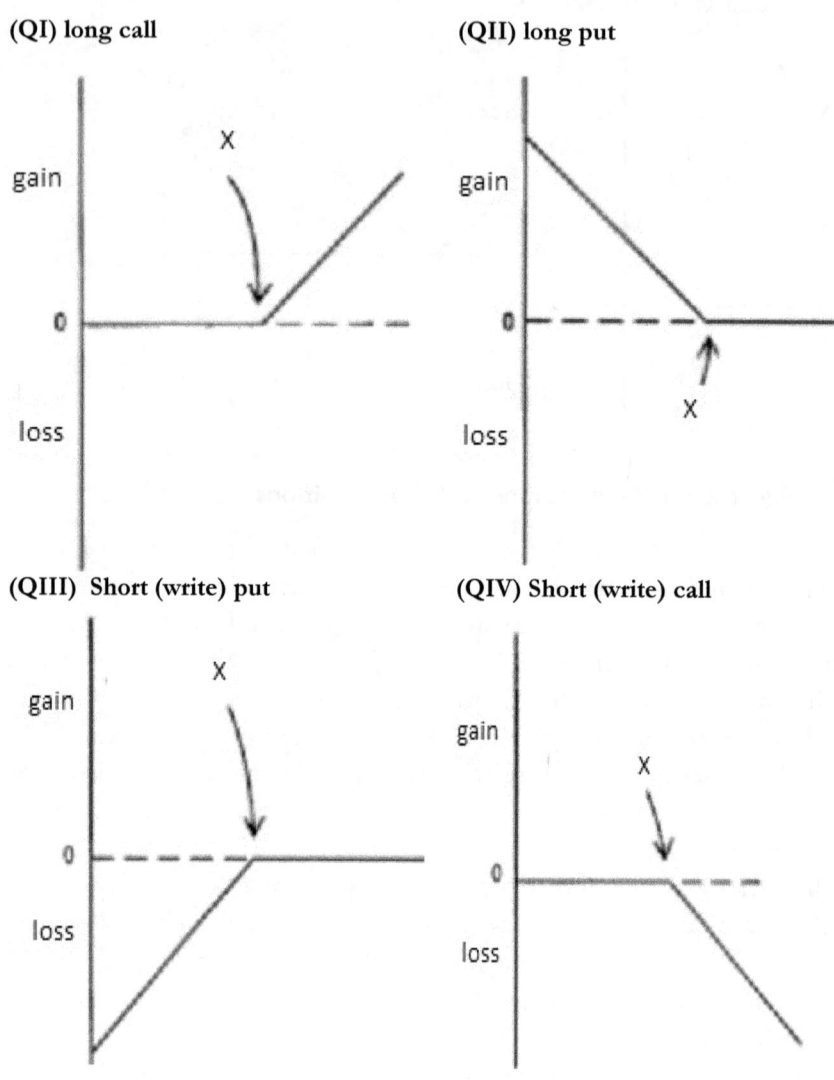

Figure 2-2. Profile of outcomes from changes in price of asset. QI and QII show long positions and QIII and QIV show short positions.

2.4.2. Premiums and excess premiums

Options do not typically sell for their minimum value. To understand why, suppose that there is a stock that sells for 20 USD at the beginning of period one and that at the end of period one it will sell for either 14 USD or 24 USD. Consider two alternatives. One is to buy 100 shares of stock and the other is to buy an option on the stock with a striking price of 20 USD. If the premium on the option is zero, would it be preferable to buy the stock or the option contract? Clearly, the answer is that buying the option is better. If the stock is purchased, either there will be a gain of 400 USD or a loss of 600 USD (we ignore commissions in these examples). But if the option is purchased and the stock increases in value to 24 USD, the option will be exercised and the gain will be 400 USD ((24-20) X 100).

On the other hand, if the stock declines in value, the option will simply expire. So if the stock increases in price, owning the option will produce the same profit as owning the stock, but if the stock falls in price, the option will have zero gain compared to a loss from owning the stock. Undoubtedly, if the premium is zero, the option is preferred. And because owning the option potentially has value since it is almost always possible that the price of the underlying asset will change so that the option will be in the money, the option premium will not be zero. This shows why options typically sell for more than their minimum value as illustrated in Figure 2.3.

Profiles of option outcomes taking premiums into account are the same as those shown in Figure 2.2 except that for the long positions the option must be subtracted from the payoff line and for short position the option must be added to the payoff line.

For warrants, the excess of the price of the warrant over its minimum value is the premium. The price of a warrant and the premium of an option are economically the same things. But there is no term for the excess of the premium on an option compared with its minimum value. This is because option terminology developed before there was a secondary market for these contracts. For lack of an alternative, we will call the difference

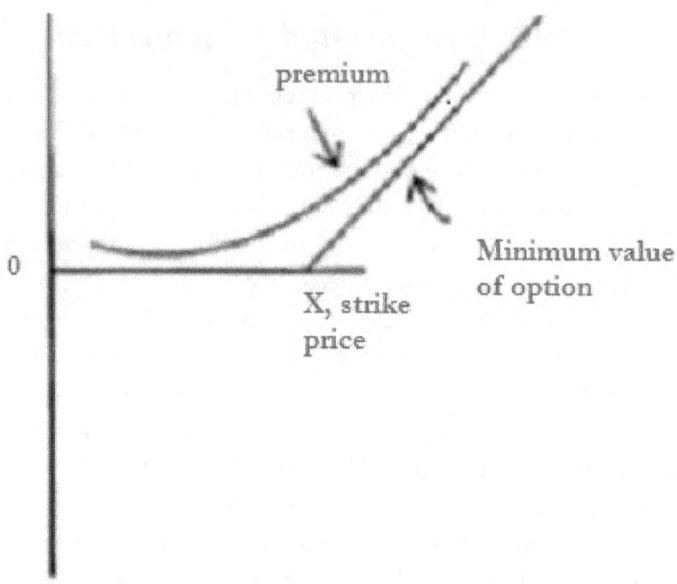

Figure 2.3. Profile of typical option premiums for given exercise price (X) as price of underlying security changes.

between the premium for an option and its minimum value the **excess premium**. Some authors refer to this excess as **time value**, but the excess premium also reflects volatility and other aspects of the option's value.

The option premium depends on five main factors. One is the rate of interest. As we have seen above the rate of interest affects the present value of the future payment or receipt when the option is exercised. However, as we will see below, generally, the effect of the rate of interest on the option premium is small. Dividends also affect option premiums. If a company pays a dividend, its stock price is reduced. If the option contract does not adjust the strike price for this reduction, the value of call options is reduced and the value of put options is increased.

Now we turn to the three most important determinants of an option's premium. For this discussion, we assume that the market rate of interest is 0%. An option's premium must be at least equal to the amount that the option is in the money. But the excess premium is generally highest with the price of the underlying asset equal the strike price. As the option becomes more and more in the money or more and more out of the money the excess premium declines.

Increased riskiness increases the value of all options. The more volatile the price of an asset the more an option on that asset is worth. As an asset's volatility increases the potential difference between the price of the underlying asset and the strike price becomes greater. Since option owners benefit from the option's potential for more extreme favorable prices, but do not suffer from more extreme unfavorable prices, options with the potential for more extreme prices are worth more. Another way of understanding this is to contemplate an option that is out of the money and whose underlying asset is so safe that its price will never change before expiration. Clearly, this option is worthless.

Finally, a longer time until expiration increases the value of all options because there is more time for the option to become in the money.

2.5. Option pricing models

There are a number of models that have been developed for pricing options and these are widely used by option professionals. We discuss two of the most popular—the binomial model and the Black-Scholes model. These two models are based on the idea that arbitrage causes assets that have the same payoffs at time t+1 to have the same value at time t. We limit our discussion to European options that do not pay dividends. American options are subject to early call, which makes the determination of their value more complicated. Likewise, options that pay dividends are more difficult to evaluate, since, among other things, the payment of a large dividend may force early exercise.

2.5.1. The binomial option pricing model

Let B represent bonds earning the risk-free rate, r. Consider the case where we have an asset selling for P_0 at $t = 0$ that has only two possible values at $t + 1$, P_u or P_d. Either the asset will be worth uP_0 or it will be worth dP_0 where u and d are values such that $uP_0 = P_u$ and $dP_0 = P_d$. Then, at $t + 1$, a call option on one unit of the asset with a striking price of P_0 will have a value at $t + 1$ of either $C_u = (uP_0 - P_0)$ or $C_d = 0$. Our goal is to form a portfolio that replicates the outcome from owning a call by borrowing at the risk-free rate and buying n units of the risky asset. In other words, if the price of the risky asset increases, we have

$$C_u = nuP_0 - B(1 + r), \tag{3}$$

and, if the price of the risky asset decreases, we have

$$C_d = ndP_0 - B(1 + r) \tag{4}$$

The variables, n, P_0 and $B(1 + r)$ have the same values in each equation. Hence, we can rearrange terms to obtain B, the amount we need to borrow, and n, the number of shares of the risk assets we need to buy, to replicate the call:

$$n = C_u - C_d / ((u - d)P_0 \tag{5}$$

$$B = (dC_u - uC_d) / ((u - d)(1 + r)) \tag{6}$$

We can illustrate these results. Let, $P_0 = 55$, $r = 0.08$, $u = 1.15$, $d = 0.9$. We can compute $P_u = 63.25$ and $P_d = 49.50$. Therefore, $C_u = uP_0 - P_0 = 63.25 - 55 = 8.25$, and $C_d = 0$. Substituting gives

$$n = (8.25 - 0) / ((1.15 - .9)55) = 0.6$$

$$B = 0.9 (8.25) / ((1.15 - 0.9)(1.08)) = 27.50$$

Owning 0.6 shares of stock and borrowing 27.50 at the risk free rate will produce, in one period, the exact same payoffs as owning one call option. Since both the stock and bond combination and the call option produce the same payoffs, they must have the same price today. Hence, the value of the call must be

$$C = nP_0 - B = .6(55) - 27.50 = 5.50$$

The accuracy of the binomial model can be improved by increasing the number of potential outcomes considered so that the model becomes multi-period. Dividing the period into smaller and smaller time intervals does this. In the two period case there are four outcomes to be analyzed. These are uu, ud, du, dd where the first item of the pair is the outcome at time t+1 and the second item is the outcome at time t+2. With the addition of more periods, the number of potential outcomes becomes very large. In general there are 2^n possible outcomes, where n is the number of period. The computational difficulty can be reduced because a number of the paths lead to the same terminal outcomes. In the two-period case the outcome ud and du produce the same terminal stock and option values so that there are only three outcomes to be evaluated.

Typically, we assume that stock returns are log normally distributed with mean μ and standard deviation σ over the time interval beginning at t and ending at T, then for large n

$$u = e^{\sigma\sqrt{(T-t)/n}} \tag{7}$$

$$d = 1/u \tag{8}$$

Further, the probability of an increase in the value of the stock at the end of any period is

$$\pi_u = ((1+r)^{(T-t)/n} - d)/(u-d) \tag{9}$$

where T - t is the proportion of a year and n is the number of periods. $\pi_d = 1 - \pi_u$. The input values for the binomial model can be estimated using historical stock returns.

Box 2-1 show how dividing the time until maturity into smaller increments works using the binomial pricing model. The example is for a European call option with a strike price of 100 when the price of the underlying asset is 100. Note the effect that dividing the interval T into two periods rather than one. When T is considered only one period, there are only two possible outcomes u, which produces a terminal value of 116.18 with probability of 0.5427, and d, which produces a terminal value of 86.07 with probability 0.4573. Dividing the interval T into two periods changes the values of u and d and increases the number of paths to uu, ud, du, and dd. Of course, ud and du produce the same terminal outcome. The increase in the number of paths and terminal outcomes considered leads to a more accurate estimate of the call's value. The process can be continued until a desired level of accuracy in comparison with the Black-Scholes model is achieved. Algorithms for calculating multi-period option values using computers have been developed and are readily available on the internet.

Box 2-1. The binomial tree

The binomial model can be used to achieve a closer and closer approximation to the Black-Scholes results by increasing the number of periods during a fixed time interval that are used to derive the binomial results. We illustrate this concept using equations 3-5 from the text. Consider a European call option with a strike price of 100 and a life of 0.25 years when the price of the underlying asset is also 100. Assume that the annual interest rate is 10% (0.10) and that the annual standard deviation is 0.3. The Black-Scholes value of the option is 10.89. We calculate the value of the call using the binomial model for 1 and 2 periods, in turn.

		n = 1	n = 2
Value		12.73	9.93
u	$e^{(0.3\sqrt{0.25})/n}$	1.1618	1.1119
d	$e^{-(0.3\sqrt{0.25})/n}$	0.8607	0.8994
π_u	$((1+.1)^{0.25}-d)/(u-d)$	0.5427	0.5299
$1-\pi_u$		0.4573	0.4701

2.5.2. Black-Scholes model

Fischer Black and Myron Scholes derived the following expression for the value of a European style call option (c):

$$c_t = P_a N(d_1) - Xe^{-r(T-t)}N(d_2)$$

where

$$d_1 = \frac{\ln\dfrac{P_a}{X} + (r+.5\sigma^2)(T-t)}{\sigma\sqrt{T-t}}$$

$$d_1 = d_2 - \sigma\sqrt{T-t}$$

N(.) = the cumulative normal distribution function, Pa is the current market price of the asset, X is the striking price of the option, σ is the standard deviation of the asset's return, r is the risk-free rate, t is the time the option is being valued, T is the time of expiration. See Box 2-2 for some examples of Black-Scholes option values.

Box 2-2. Estimating Black-Scholes option values

We use the program found at the following web site http://www.ggw.org/donorware/options/ to calculate the Black-Scholes option values for a European call option with a strike price of 100, two month life, $(T - t) = 0.166$, a standard deviation of 0.3, and an interest rate or 0.05. The option premiums calculated for each of the follow values of the underlying asset are:

Price of underlying asset	Option premium	Intrinsic value = minimum value	Excess of premium over intrinsic value
120	21.21	19.83	1.38
110	12.17	9.92	2.25
100	5.20	0	5.20
90	1.36	0	1.36
80	0.24	0	0.24

As a practical matter, the current stock price, Pa, the strike price X, the risk-free rate r, and the time remaining until the option expires, (T-t) are known. Only the volatility, σ, that will occur for the stock over the remaining life of the option needs to be estimated in order to find the theoretical price of a call option. Put-call parity allows for the pricing of the matching put option, once the value for the call option has been assigned. Differences in the estimate of future volatility will lead to different prices for an option.

On the other hand, options trade all the time and the price they trade at can be found on many financial web sites. Knowing the determinants of an option's value and the options current market price, c, a value for σ can be obtained using the Black-Scholes formula. This volatility value obtained from the options market is called implied volatility.

There has been a great deal of work to extend the Black-Scholes model to remedy its limitations. Merton (1976) demonstrated how the model could be adjusted to account for dividends that were paid continuously. MacBeth and Merville (1979) found that the model systematically under priced in the money options and overpriced out-of-the-money options. Moreover, these biases tended to be greater the longer the life of the option. However, the fact that the Black-Scholes model cannot price American style options on dividend paying stocks remains an important limitation.

In 1993 the Chicago Board of Exchange introduced the CBOE volatility index, which has the ticker symbol VIX, as a new index of implied volatility for the US equity market.

In March 2003 the CBOE introduced a new VIX formula, which calculates the VIX as a weighted sum of out-of-the-money prices across all available strike prices on the S&P 500 index. The CBOE methodology allows the calculation of the index without using the Black-Scholes formula. The VIX is often referred to in the popular and financial press as the 'fear index.' The index represents the predicted volatility of the S&P 500 over the next 30 days and is calculated in real time, throughout the trading day. The VIX index changes frequently and by significant amounts (see Figure 2-4).[1]

2.5.3. Option Greeks

Option Greeks are very important to investment professionals because they are used in hedging risk.[2] [3] They express how option value change when one of the inputs into the Black-Scholes Option Pricing Model changes, holding the other inputs constant. The formulas for the Greeks are obtained using calculus and can differ for puts and calls. We consider only options on non-dividend paying assets.

---

[1] For a discussion of the VIX index see Fleming, Ostdiek, and Whaley (1994) and Bittman (1998) and Zhu and Lian (2012). A layman's overview of how the VIX is calculated is provided at: http://www.investopedia.com/articles/active-trading/070213/tracking-volatility-how-vix-calculated.asp;
and; http://onlyvix.blogspot.com/2011/09/intuitive-understanding-of-vix-formula.html

[2] The following web site provide programs for calculating option Greeks: http://www.volatilitytrading.net/optioncalculator.htm

[3] http://en.wikipedia.org/wiki/Greeks_(finance)

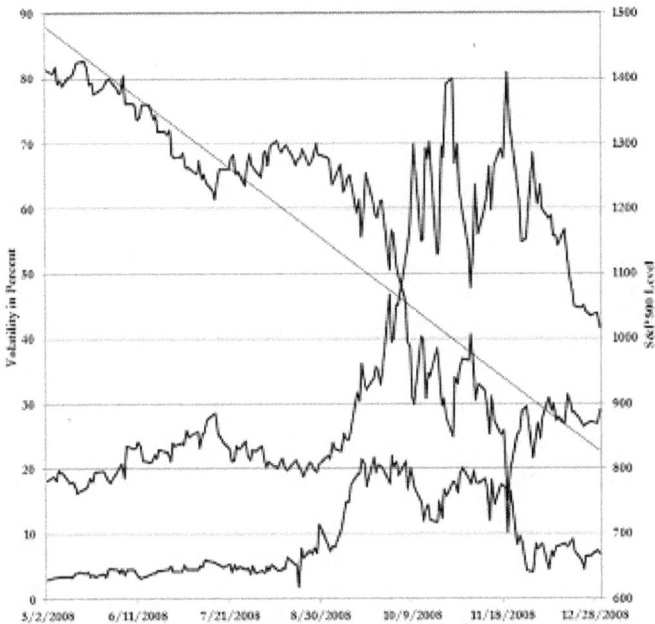

From top to bottom near left axis: (1) S&P trend, (2) S&P 500, (3) VIX volatility, and (4) estimated volatility

Figure 2-4. VIX volatility vs. estimated volatility for the S&P 500

Delta is the rate of change in the price of an option in response to a change in the value of the underlying asset. The delta for a call is $\partial c / \partial S = N(d_1)$.[1] The delta of a call option is positive because an increase in the price of the underlying asset increases the value of the option. Call options that are deep in the money have deltas that are close to 1.0 because the value of the option increases by almost exactly the same amount as the value of the underlying stock. Call options that are deep out of the money have deltas that are positive, but small. Put option deltas are negative because a decrease in the value of the underlying asset reduces the value of the option. The delta is close to -1 for deep in the money put options and close to 0 for deep out of the money put options. When an option is deep out of

---

[1] The formulas for the other Greeks considered here are quite complicated and we do not present them. They can be found in standard options texts such as Kolb (1997).

the money a large change in the value of the stock produces a small absolute change in the value of the option, giving a small delta. The delta for a long and short position in an underlying asset is +1 and –1, respectively.

Gamma is the only Greek that does not measure option premium sensitivity to a change in one of the Black-Scholes inputs. Rather gamma measures the rate of change in an option's delta in response to a change in the price of the underlying asset. An option's gamma is largest when the option is at the money. Both puts and calls have positive gammas. For a given gamma, an increase in a stock's price produces a larger profit than a decrease in a stock's price of the same size.

Theta is the rate of change in the value of an option related to the change in the length of time until its expiration. A negative theta indicates that the value of an option position is declining through time. As an option becomes more in the money or out-of-the-money, theta tends toward zero. For an at the money option call theta declines gradually when maturity is distant, but declines more and more rapidly as maturity gets closer and closer.

Vega is the rate of change of the value of an option with the respect to the volatility of the underlying asset.[1] Puts and calls have the same vega, which is always positive. Long positions benefit from an increase in volatility. Vega is a major determinant of an option's value and a change in vega can significantly change the option premium.

Rho is the rate of change of the value of the option with respect to interest rates. Rho is always positive for calls and always negative for puts. Large changes in interest rates do not have much effect on option values

The Greeks are useful in constructing portfolios that have a desired exposure to particular determinants of an option's determinants.

Consider an American call option and an American put option on a non-dividend paying stock with a striking price of 50 when the price of the underlying asset is 50. Assume that the market rate of interest is 0%, volatility is 20% per year, and the maturity of the option is 30 days. The value of a call, the value of a put, and the Greeks for each of these options are presented in Table 2-1.

---

[1] Note that vega is not a Greek letter.

$$nc = 0.96 \, np$$

Hence, for American options on a non-dividend paying stock when interest rates are 0%, buying 100 calls and 100 puts with the same strike price and maturity produces a portfolio with a delta of 0. Likewise, writing 100 of these same puts and 100 of these calls also produces a portfolio with a delta of 0.

Table 2-1. The option value and Greeks for a put and call.

This table presents the Black-Scholes option value and the Greeks for a European call and put with a life of 30 days and a strike price of 50. The price of the asset is 50, the interest rate is 0%, the volatility is 20% per year, and the asset does not pay a dividend.

	Call	Put
Value of option (premium)	1.134	1.134
Delta	0.511	-0.489
Gamma	0.136	0.136
Theta	-0.141	-0.141
Vega	0.057	0.057
Rho	0.02	-0.018

Source: http://www.cboe.com/LearnCenter/OptionCalculator.aspx

Note that when interest rates are 0% and the asset does not pay a dividend, the premium on the call and the put are the same. This reflects the fact that we measure risk using standard deviation, which gives symmetric outcomes. The prospect of any particular positive return is mirrored by an equally likely negative return.

Suppose that a trader wishes to construct a portfolio comprising calls and stock such that the delta of the portfolio is 0. Let nc = the number of calls each covering 100 shares, np = the number of puts each covering 100 shares, ns = the number of 100-share lots of the stock, and δc and δc = the delta of the call and stock, respectively. Then we seek:

$$B = 0.9 \, (8.25)/((1.15 - 0.9)(1.08)) = 27.50$$

We know that the delta for a long stock position is 1. Letting nc = 1 and noting that δc = 0.511 and solving, we obtain ns = -0.511. For each call owned 51.1 shares of stock must be shorted to achieve a portfolio with a 0 delta. If the portfolio has a delta of 0, for small changes in the value of the stock, the value of the option-stock portfolio does not change.

Next consider zero-delta portfolios constructed by owning or writing calls and puts. Noting that $\delta p = -0.489$ and $\delta c = 0.511$, we have

$$0.511nc - 0.489np = 0$$

Rearranging and dividing by 0.511 gives

The vega of a portfolio of puts and call that have identical characteristics is

$$np\ vp + nc\ vc$$

which simplifies to $(np + nc)$ since $vp = vc$. Hence, if a trader owns a call and put with otherwise identical characteristics, the vega of portfolio is $0.057 + 0.057 = 0.114$. But the vega of a portfolio formed by writing these two options is -0.114. Hence, we can see that two portfolios that have identical delta's may not have identical vega's. In fact, the vega's of the two portfolios are dramatically different. If a trader expected volatility to increase ceteris paribus, the trader would buy calls and puts. But if the trader expects volatility to decrease the trader would write calls and puts.

2.6. Exercising options

2.6.1. Exercising options versus closing out positions

At the maturity of an option contract, the excess premium is zero and the option is worth its minimum value. Also, ignoring commissions, the amount received when an option is exercised is the option's minimum value. To see this, consider a call option with a striking price of 20 whose underlying security is selling for 22. Upon exercise, assuming that the option requires delivery rather cash settlement, the owner receives the underlying security, which has a value of 22, but pays a price of 20. When the underlying security is sold for 22, the purchase price is recouped plus an additional 2. This is, of course, equal to the amount the option is in the money, 22 minus 10.

In most cases there is an incentive for both the writer and the owner of an exchange-traded option to close out the position at expiration rather than exercise the option. Upon exercise the owner of a call pays the striking price plus commission and receives the underlying asset. If the owner sells the asset another commission is paid. Thus, in exercising an option an owner may pay two commissions on the underlying interest—one at the striking price and one at the market price. Typically, it is more economical to just sell the option.

The writer has similar motives for closing out the position rather than waiting for it to be exercised. If the call writer is covered, then the stock is sold to the option owner at the striking price less commission and must be replaced at the current market price plus commission. If the writer is uncovered, the asset must be purchased for delivery at the market price plus commission and delivered at the striking price less commission. In either case, the writer incurs two commissions. Therefore, for the writer too, it is typically more economical to close out the position rather than exercise.

2.6.2. Exercising exchange-traded options

We have seen that if an option is exercised, ignoring commission, the economic value realized by the owner is the amount that the option is in the money. Because most options have positive excess premiums, meaning that the premium is more that the option's minimum value, owners of options rarely exercise except at expiration when the excess premium become zero. If an option is deep in the money or deep out of the money the excess premium may also disappear.

Dividends can also result in the early exercise of American style call options. Suppose that an investor owns an American exchange-traded call option. If a large dividend is declared on the underlying security, it may make sense to exercise because dividends go to the owner of the security on the record date. Consider a call option on 100 shares of stock selling for 52 with a strike price of 50 and with an excess premium of 1. In this case, the premium is 3, the sum of the amount the option is in the money and the excess premium. Suppose that the company announces a dividend on this stock of 4. Thus, when this stock goes ex dividend, ceteris paribus, the stock will be worth 48 and the option will be worth the amount that it is in the money, 0, plus the excess premium. If the excess premium does not fall, the post-dividend option premium will be 1. So if the owner does nothing, the value of the owner's option will fall from 3 to 1. But if the option is exercised prior to the dividend the owner pays for 50 for the shares that can be sold for 52, realizing 2. Hence, in this case it is better to exercise.

Some readers may ask why not just sell the option for 3. The answer is that once the firm announces the forthcoming dividend the option will no longer be worth 3, but rather its price will decline to 2. Thus, the owner of the option at the time the dividend is announced realizes the loss. Typically, this is only a problem for dividend-paying stocks if the amount of the dividend is large and unexpected.

For American exchange-traded put options, if the earnings from investing the amount realized upon exercise is greater than the expected profit from continuing to hold the option, the excess premium may disappear and it may make sense to exercise. From a legal perspective, whether or not an option is exercised is at the discretion of the owner of the contract. But from an economic perspective either the writer or owner can decide whether the option will be exercised. To understand this concept, consider a call option that is expiring in the money. If the writer does not close out the contract prior to expiration, the owner is forced to exercise because that is the only way to realize the minimum value. Naturally, any particular owner can sell their contract. But if an option is in the money at expiration and if a writer does not close out a position, some owner will be forced to exercise.

There might be a number of reasons that either an owner or writer desires to exercise. Perhaps the owner of an in the money call or the writer of an in the money put simply desires to own the underlying asset. Other considerations may also apply. For an actual case see Box 2-3.

2.6.3. *Exercising over-the-counter options*

Suppose the owner of an over-the-counter call option expects a short-lived downturn in the market and wishes to protect the position temporarily. Since there is probably no secondary market for the option, one possibility is to exercise the option. Of course, this is only feasible if the option is in the money. Further, exercise sacrifices the excess premium. Another approach is to hedge by buying a put or writing a call on an exchange.

Box 2-3. Should this put be exercised or closed out?

The author was involved in the management of a small investment portfolio that purchased 3,000 shares of common stock in a firm we will call ABC Industries at 30 (excluding commission). The stock advanced to 36. Believing that the stock would go higher, we placed a limit order to sell (write) 10 put options with a striking price of 35 at a premium of 0.75. Each option covered 100 shares of ABC. The broker was instructed to sell the options one at a time or in any increments of 1 (some traders prefer to limit their trades to a certain number of contracts or more, but we decided not to do this). At the end of the day one contract had been sold. The proceeds were 0.75 per share less commission of 0.35 per share. Thus, the aggregate net proceeds were only ((0.75 - 0.35 X 100) 40 USD. The failure to sell all of the contracts combined with the high commission on just one contract made this transaction unexpectedly poor from the first day. But things got worse. Instead of rising, the price of ABC fell to 34 on expiration day. Now we were faced with the choice of (1) repurchasing the put contract, or (2) doing nothing and waiting until the owner of the contract exercised, in which case we would acquire 100 shares of ABC at 35 USD each plus commission. What would you do?

Answer: There is no right or wrong answer. Some managers might exercise and some might not. We decided not to close out the position, which forced the owner to exercise.

1. If the option-writing strategy is chosen the manager has incurred a loss of 40 USD, an inconsequential amount of money. But the transaction will likely be enumerated separately, distracting from an otherwise excellent performance.

2. If the option is allowed to expire in the money, the option will be exercised and 100 shares of the underlying stock will be purchased for the account. How will the account look then? The cost of the 100 shares is 3,500 plus a commission of, say, 25. Now the fund owns 3,100 shares with a cost of 30.17 and a market value of 34. No loss is ever realized to detract attention from the overall profit on this trade.

We have already seen circumstances such as when a large dividend is declared to when the value of a put makes it more valuable dead than alive in which the owner of an exchange traded option would exercise early. In general, the owner of a over-the-counter option would exercise under these same circumstances as long as the terms of the two options were comparable. Historically, the striking price for an over-the counter option was reduced by the amount of a dividend on the ex-dividend date. Such a contract term would affect the desirability of exercising prior to a dividend.

3. Option strategies

3.1. Reasons for owning and writing options

There are three primary reasons for owning options:

1. Many firms and individuals use options to speculate because of the leverage they provide. For a premium that is typically small in relation to the value of the underlying interest an investor profits from the change in price of 100 shares of the underlying security.

2. A second reason for using options rather than other types of financial instruments is that the loss is limited to the initial payment, the premium. At first it might seem strange that only being able to lose the entire investment is an advantage. But with some other types of financial instruments, such as futures and buying stock on margin, an investor can lose more than the initial investment. While the loss is also limited for stocks and bonds, these instruments require a much larger initial outlay to generate the same profit potential.

3. Options are useful in meeting many of the needs of hedgers.

There are also three primary option writing strategies:

1. Option writing can be used to speculate on a price decrease in the underlying asset. Suppose that an investor expects the price of AUD to fall relative to the USD. One alternative is to short a futures contract on AUD. Another is to enter into a forward contract to sell AUD. A third alternative is to write a call on AUD. If no offsetting position is held in the underlying asset or in an equivalent such as a convertible security or another option, the writer is naked or uncovered. If the price of AUD falls relative to the USD, then the premium on the contract should also fall. In fact, if there is a positive excess premium, then the premium must fall over time unless the

price of the underlying asset increases. By contrast, if a put option is purchased, the price of the underlying asset typically must fall for the owner to have a gain.

2. Like owning options, writing options can be used in hedging strategies.

3. A third reason for writing options is to earn income. The investor writes a call option on an asset that the investors owns, which is called **covered** writing. If the position is held until expiration, the investor keeps the entire premium. However, if the option is in the money at expiration the investor has incurred an opportunity cost of the amount that the option is in the money. And if the option is out of the money at expiration the investor's gain is reduced by the amount that the option is out of the money.

Suppose that an investor owns 100 shares of the U.S. firm International Business Machines (IBM) which is selling at 56 and that a call option on IBM with an expiration in two months and a striking price of 55 has a premium of 2.5. By selling this call, the investor receives 250 less commission. It is usually possible to get a clear picture of what could happen by assuming that the option is held to maturity, and, then, considering the results of only a few outcomes. In this case four possible outcomes are of interest:[2]

1. the option is out of the money at expiration. The investor's loss on the long position in the underlying stock will be 56 minus the stock's price. If the loss on the stock is greater than the 2.5 received as the premium, the overall outcome will be a loss.

2. the option is at the money at expiration. The investor will have a loss of 1 on the underlying stock. This loss will only partially offset the option premium so that the overall result is a 1.5 gain.

3. the price of the underlying asset has not changed at expiration. The writer can buy back the option for 1. Or the writer can wait for the owner to exercise and sell the stock, which is currently worth 56 for the striking price of 55. Since we are ignoring commissions, these two actions are equivalent. In either case the writer incurs a loss of 1 that will offset part of the premium received initially, so that the overall outcome is a gain of 1.5.

---

[2] We ignore commissions in these examples.

4. the value of the underlying security has increased. The investor will have a gain on the stock position, but a loss on the option position. Suppose that the stock increases in value to 60. There will be a (60 - 56 =) 4 gain from the ownership position in the stock. But the option will be 5 in the money at expiration so that the option position produces a loss of (5 - 2.50) = 2.5. Hence, the overall outcome is a gain of 1.5.

In general, the writer of a covered option earns the entire excess premium if the option closes either at or in the money. But if the option closes out of the money, the writer earns the entire premium less any loss on the underlying security. Thus, in this case, if the option is at or in the money at maturity there will be a gain of 1.5, but if the option is out of the money the outcome will be: (price of underlying asset - 56) + 2.5.

3.2. Risks of owning and writing options

The most important risk of owning an option is the possibility of losing one's entire premium in a very short period of time. The author once met a broker who decided to purchase an option for his own account. The broker walked from his desk to the firm's clerk and handed in the order for transmission to the firm's trading desk. Before the broker had time to return to his desk there was an announcement that reduced the value of the option to almost zero. Clearly, the time needed for an investor to lose his/her entire investment can be very short in the options market.

Uncovered writers face the possibility of essentially unlimited loss from an unfavorable move in the price of the underlying asset. Covered writers face the risk of losing their entire investment in the underlying asset.

Writers can be assigned unwanted exercise notices. Trading in either the underlying asset or the option itself may be halted by the exchanges. There are other risks, but these mostly have to do with potential problems in the operations of the options markets.

3.3. Option spreads and straddles

3.3.1. Spreads

It is common on an exchange to have many different options trading on the same underlying asset at the same time. These options differ in either striking price or in expiration date. Some traders enter into strategies involving a **spread**, the simultaneous purchase of one option contract and the sale of another. A **bull** spread is profitable if the price of the underlying asset increases and a **bear** spread is profitable if the price of the underlying asset declines. If the spread is profitable when the price does not change, it is a **neutral** spread.

If the two options involved in a spread have different expiration dates, the spread is a **time** or **calendar** spread. If the longer-lived option is purchased and the shorter-lived option is sold, the spreader hopes that the time value of the shorter-lived option will fall faster than that of the longer option. This is most likely to happen if the price of the underlying stock either does not change or falls. There probably will be no margin required on this strategy because the short position is fully covered by the long position. Also, the premium on the longer-lived asset will be larger than the premium on the shorter lived asset, so that the spreader will have to pay the difference when the spread is initiated.

If the two options involved are of the same maturity, but differ in striking price, the spread is a **price spread**. For calls, if the option with the lower striking price is bought and the option with the higher striking price is sold, the spreader will profit from an increase in the price of the underlying asset above the lower striking price until the higher striking price is reached. This is a bull spread. Since the long option position provides protection for the short position, there will likely be no margin on this transaction. But the spreader will have to pay the difference in the two premiums when the spread is initiated.

It is difficult to make profits on spreads for several reasons. One is that the transaction costs are high. There are two commissions at the outset and two more commissions later unless the options expire out of the money. Also, there are bid-ask spreads that are incurred on both **legs** (the purchase and sale at the initiation of the spread are the two legs). An additional difficulty is that the spreader must be careful that both legs of the spread are executed at the same time. Otherwise the spreader will have exposure on one leg.

3.3.2. Straddles

The change in an option's value with respect to a change in the volatility of the underlying asset is known as the option's **vega**. A **straddle** or **volatility** spread involves the purchase of both a put and call on the same stock or the sale of both a put and a call on the same stock. If the put and call are purchased, the spread is long volatility. In other words, an increase in the riskiness of the underlying asset will increase the value of both options. If both the put and the call are written, the position is short volatility so that an increase in the riskiness of the underlying asset will decrease the value of both options. We presented an example of these two spreads above.

4. Options on individual stocks, futures, and indexes

The underlying interests for options are varied. The most common option types are on individual stocks, futures contracts, and indexes. We will examine specific examples of each of these types of options.

4.1. Equity options on individual stocks

Options on individual stocks are traded on many exchanges including the Chicago Board Options Exchange. The CBOE options are American options that cover 100 shares, unless an adjustment for a stock split or stock dividend has been required. Both puts and calls are traded. For each stock, options are traded on the nearest two months and on quarterly cycles. Each underlying stock is assigned to one of three cycles: (1) January-April-July-October, (2) February-May-August-November, or (3) March-June-September-December. The last trading day is the third Friday of the expiration month and the options expire the next day. Based on the trading price of the underlying stock, the increments of striking prices used are USD 2.50 for prices of USD 25 or less, USD 5 for prices up to 200, and USD 10 for prices over USD 200. Settlement is by delivery of the underlying stock. Initially, the striking prices straddle the price of the underlying stock. As the price of the stock changes new striking prices are added so that there is at least one option with a striking price above and one with a striking price below the current price of the underlying asset. Of course, the options that had previously begun trading continue to trade.

4.2. Options on futures

Put and call options on the futures contract on the MSCI Singapore Free Index traded on the Singapore Exchange. The MSCI Singapore Free Index is a capitalization weighted index that tracks the performance of stocks listed on the Singapore Exchange. The index weights are adjusted to reflect free float, which are shares that can be freely traded. [1]

4.3. Index options

The Hong Kong Exchange lists European puts and calls on an index of Hong Kong stocks. Expiration dates for nearby months and some further out months are traded. The contract size is 50 HKD per index point. The index's all-time closing high of 31,958.41 was set on 30 October 2007. The tick size is one index point. The options expire on the penultimate business date of the contract month. There is no physical delivery; the contract is settled in cash.[2]

4.4. Weather-linked options

Insurance companies face a problem in providing coverage for low-frequency, high-severity losses. Facing the possibility of a catastrophic loss, insurance companies can purchase reinsurance from other companies or maintain large amounts of capital. The occurrence of two major natural catastrophes in the U.S., Hurricane Andrew in 1992 and the Northridge earthquake in 1994 severely diminished the availability of reinsurance. Insurance companies are not the only ones facing weather-related risk. Utilities face increased costs for raw materials if a winter is unusually cold

---

[1]
http://www.sgx.com/wps/wcm/connect/e203978047979271b089b0cb70e00a63/SGX+MSCI+Singapore+Options+Contract+Specifications.pdf?MOD=AJPERES&CACHEID=e203978047979271b089b0cb70e00a63

[2]
http://www.hkex.com.hk/eng/global/faq/Documents/options_table.pdf

or a summer is unusually hot. Farmers and others dealing with agricultural commodities also face risks associated with the weather.

Various option products have been developed to deal with these risks. The CME Group offers temperature-related options for many U.S. cities and other cities throughout the world. Contracts also cover frost, snowfall, and rainfall.[1] There are two types of temperature measures, cooling degree days (CDD) and heating degree days (HDD). For a given day, calculate D = the absolute value of (average temperature - 65 degrees Fahrenheit). If the average temperature is less than 65 degrees Fahrenheit, D = the number of HDDs; otherwise, D is the number of CDDs. Over the course of a month both CDDs and HDDs may accumulate. Weather options are based on the cumulative HDDs and CDDs over a period such as a month. CDDs and HDDs spanning a number of months with a specified strike price for each month, called **strips**, are also traded. A strip might cover the cooling season of April through October. A heating oil retailer may purchase an option to protect against an unusually warm winter. If the winter is warm, the retailer will have a gain on the option. If the winter is cold, the retailer will have a loss on the option, but this will be offset to some extent by good profits from the sale of heating oil.

In the traditional reinsurance market, one insurance company can examine the specific risks of another insurance company and assess the nature and extent of the risks faced. This makes the issuance of a reinsurance policy covering this specific risk possible. Because it would be difficult for investors to evaluate the potential losses from the policies of an individual firm, derivatives based on the policies of an individual company are not likely to be viable. An alternative is to use an index that reflects industry-wide loss experience. Illustrating this approach, the CME Group offers hurricane-related options based on the CME Hurricane Index™.[2]

Both hedgers and speculators are needed to make these contracts successful. Insurance companies, reinsurance companies, utilities and others can trade these contracts among themselves, providing price-discovery and risk transfer benefits. But without speculators, new capital is not attracted to the market. One difficulty in attracting speculators to these markets is

---

[1] http://www.cmegroup.com/trading/weather/index.html

[2] http://www.cmegroup.com/rulebook/CME/IV/400/431B/431B.pdf

that the Black-Scholes option pricing model cannot be use to value options because the underlying interest is not a traded asset.[1]

5. Summary

There are two parties to each options contract, the owner and the writer. For calls, the owner has the right, if he/she chooses, to purchase an underlying interest from the writer at a stated price, the striking price. For puts, the owner has the right, if he/she chooses, to sell an underlying interest to the writer at the striking price. Options terminate on the expiration date. If the option is American, it can be exercised at any time, but if it is European, it can only be exercised at maturity. Some contracts provide for a settlement in cash rather than physical delivery. Writers are covered if they have an offsetting position in the underlying security or its equivalent. Otherwise they are naked.

Option positions can be taken in either the over-the-counter or listed markets. Exchange-traded options are standardized. All contracts are with an intermediary such as the Option Clearing Corporation in the U.S. Individual writers and owners are only matched upon exercise. Only the price of the option, the premium, is negotiated on the exchange. The types of orders that can be placed and the way option trades are executed on exchanges is essentially the same as for stocks. The Chicago Board Options Exchange has designated market makers.

The minimum value of an option is the amount that the option is in the money, but cannot be negative. The premium for an option is the sum of an option's minimum value and its excess premium. The value of the excess premium is affected by a number of factors including (1) the riskiness of the underlying security, (2) the life of the option, (3) the extent to which the option is in or out of the money, (4) the cost of carrying the underlying interest, (5) potential gains from exercise, and (6) the level of interest rates.

The margin on the purchase of an option contract is usually 100%. Covered writers typically do not post margin, while the level of margin required for naked writers is usually based on the value of the underlying interest.

---

[1] Canter, Cole, and Sandor (1996).

The change in the price of an option in response to a change in the value of the underlying asset is called the option's delta. The delta of a call option is positive. Gamma is the change in an option's delta in response to a change in the price of the underlying asset. An option's gamma is largest when the option is at the money.

Upon exercise, the economic value of the owner's position is the amount the option is in the money less commissions. Because most options have a positive excess premium, American options are usually exercised near expiration, if at all. It is usually more economical for both the owner and the writer of an option to close out the position rather than to exercise.

Ownership of options is attractive to many investors because of the leverage they provide and because the loss is limited to the amount of the premium. Writers can speculate on price changes in the underlying asset or seek to earn premium income. Both owners and writers use options for hedging.

The owner of an option risks losing the entire premium in a short period of time. The writer of an option faces the prospect of loss due to an unfavorable price movement in the underlying asset.

Some investors enter into a spread, the simultaneous purchase of one option contract and sale of another. If the two options involved in a spread have different expiration dates, the spread is a calendar spread. If the two options involved have the same maturity, but differ in striking price, the spread is a price spread.

Questions

1. What is the difference between a call option and a put option? For the put and call, which party has an obligation to make delivery if the option is exercised?
2. For options with the same basic features, explain whether an American option is more valuable than a European option.
3. Define each of the option Greeks.
4. Define open interest.
5. Why might one want to use a limit order rather than a market order when initiating new positions in options on individual stocks?

6. When is a put option in-the-money, out-of-the-money, and at-the-money?
7. Why is an uncovered option position riskier than a covered position?
8. What determines the amount of the option premium?
9. What are the main reasons for owning options? Writing options?
10. What is the difference between a time and a price spread?

References

Bittman, James B., 1998, Trading Index Options. New York: McGraw-Hill.

Canter, Michael S., Joseph B. Cole, and Richard L. Sandor, 1996, Insurance derivatives: a new asset class for the capital markets and a new hedging tool for the insurance industry, Journal of Derivatives 4, 89-104.

Fleming, Jeff, Barbara Ostdiek, and Robert E. Whaley, 1994, Predicting stock market volatility: a new measure, Working paper, Duke University, Durham, NC.

Knoll, Michael S., 194, Put-call parity and the law, Working paper, Los Angeles: University of Southern California.

Kolb, Robert W., 1997, Futures, Options and Swaps. Oxford: Blackwell.

Litzenberger, Robert H., David R. Beaglehole, and Craig E. Reynolds, 1996, Assessing catastrophe reinsurance-linked securities as a new asset class, Journal of Portfolio Management 76-86.

Sears, Steven M., 1999, Philadelphia exchange to reduce fees for options transactions, Wall Street Journal, February 8.

Zhu, Song-Ping, and Guang-Hua Lian, 2012, An analytical formula for VIX futures and its applications, Journal of Futures Markets 32, 166-190.

CHAPTER THREE

SWAPS

Key Terms

Accreting swaps—a swap for which the notional principal increases at one or more times during the tenor of the swap.

Actuals—any assets that are exchanged at the effective date.

All-in cost--the total cost of a financial transaction including underwriting fees, interest expenses, and servicing costs.

Amortizing swaps--a swap for which the notional principal decreases at one or more points during the tenor of the contract.

Bucketing—the practice in which a firm assuming the counterparty risk for customer orders itself rather than executing these orders on an exchange.

Buckets—a period used to aggregate cash flows for assessing swaps.

Bucket shops—firms that regularly bucket customer orders.

Bond equivalent yield differential—an adjustment used to standardize interest raters on instruments ordinarily quoted on a bank discount basis.

Buy down—a swap with an initial fixed-rate below the market rate, requiring a payment by the fixed-rate payer.

Buy up—a swap with an initial fixed-rate coupon above the market rates, requiring a payment by the floating-rate counterparty.

Cap—a pre-specified maximum rate that will be paid on a swap.

Collar—a swap with both a floor and cap.

Counterparty—the parties to a swap.

Delayed-rate-setting swaps—a swap that commences immediately, but for which the coupon rate is set later according to a procedure specified in the swap agreement.

Effective date—the date on which a swap commences.

Fixed-for-floating—one counterparty pays a fixed rate and the other pays a variable rate.

Floating rate—a variable rate used to calculate periodic payments on a swap.

Floor—places a limit on the minimum rate that will be paid.

Law of comparative advantage—producers should specialize in the items for which they have the lowest opportunity cost.

Macrohedge—hedging using a portfolio approach rather than swap by swap.

Maturity date—the date on which a swap ends.

Money market equivalent yield differential—a method of quoting LIBOR rates based on *actual days / 360 days*.

Notional assets—fictional amounts used to calculate the value of payments required during the life of a swap.

Off-market swaps—swaps with a nonzero initial net present value.

Participating forwards—a swap with either a fixed cap and a flexible floor or a fixed floor and a flexible cap.

Par swap—a swap for which the fixed and floating legs have about the same present value so that the net present value of the contract is zero.

Payment dates—the date on which swap payments occur.

Plain vanilla—the basic form of a swap.

Range forwards—a swap combining a long cap with a short floor.

Reference rate—a cash market rate used to calculate the floating rate payments for a swap.

Reset dates—the date on which a reference rate is observed.

Reversible swaps—a swap in which the counterparties switch roles as the fixed- and floating receiver.

Roller coaster swap—a swap that allows for both increases and decreases in notional principal.

Seasonal swaps—a swap designed to deseason a firm's cash flows.

Swap—a contract evidenced by a single document in which two parties agree to exchange periodic payments.

Swap book—the portfolio of swaps.

Swap coupon—the fixed rate used to calculate periodic payments on a swap.

Swaptions—an option on a swap, giving the holder the right to enter into a swap at a later date.

Tenor—the life of a swap.

Termination clauses—provisions of a swap contract detailing how losses are determined in the event of default.

Termination date—the date on which a swap ends.

Value date—the date on which a swap commences.

Zero coupon swaps—a swap with a fixed rate swap coupon that is zero.

IN THIS CHAPTER, we explain how swaps work. Specifically, we explore
- basic interest rate, currency, and commodity swaps,
- variations on these swap types,
- options on swaps, and
- the economics and valuation of swaps.

We also discuss the reasons for the development of the swaps market and the creation and management of swaps. Specifically, we describe
- the way swaps are used,
- the role of swap dealers, and
- the management of swap risk.

1. Introduction

Swaps are the most recent innovation in derivatives. Since their development in the 1980s the notional value of swaps has grown rapidly. Today swaps are well established and have become standard tools used by commercial firms, institutional investors, and banks. Swaps are used in such varied applications as restructuring a firm's balance sheet, changing an investor's asset allocation and protecting a producer from inventory price risk. The two most common type of swaps are interest rate swaps and currency swaps. As of the end of December 2014 the notional value of all swaps outstanding was 614 trillion USD. Clearly a market this large demands the attention of students of finance.

2. Types of swaps

A **swap** is a contract evidenced by a single document in which two parties agree to exchange periodic payments. In some cases, assets are also exchanged at the beginning and end of the swap. The contract commences on its **effective date** or **value date** and ends on its **maturity date** or **termination date**. The two parties to a swap are called **counterparties**. **Actuals** are assets that are exchanged at the effective date. If no assets are exchanged at the effective date, then fictional amounts, called **notional assets** or notional principal, are used to calculate the value of payments required during the life or **tenor** of the swap agreement. A notional asset is not really an asset. Instead, it is an amount used to calculate swap payments.

There are three major categories of swaps: interest rate, currency, and commodity. Each of these has a basic form, often referred to as **plain vanilla**, and an almost limitless number of variations.

2.1. Plain vanilla swaps

2.1.1. Interest rate swaps

In a plain vanilla interest rate swap, one party pays, and the other receives, periodic payments of the net of:

(1) a fixed rate of interest, the **swap coupon**, on a stated amount of debt

less

(2) a variable or **floating rate** of interest on the same given amount of debt.

This is called a **fixed-for-floating** swap. Since the amount of debt covered by the fixed and floating rates is the same, there is no need to exchange the actual debt at either the effective date or at maturity. In other words, the debt is a notional amount, used simply to determine the periodic interest payments. Note that (1) minus (2) can be either positive or negative, so that either party may actually be required to make the payment. Likewise, either party may actually receive the payment. The counterparties can agree to make these payments monthly, semiannually, yearly, or at other times.

The floating rate is based on a specific cash market rate, the **reference rate**, which is observed on specific dates, the **reset dates**. Payments occur on the **payment dates**. Floating rates such as LIBOR plus a stated percentage (e.g., LIBOR + 2.5%) or the yield on a U.S. Treasury note of comparable tenor plus a stated percentage are common. **All-in cost** is the total cost of a swap transaction including underwriting fees, interest expenses, and servicing costs. The all-in cost is often stated as an annual percentage rate, payable semiannually. The all-in cost is typically quoted against LBOR flat. **Flat** means that the LBOR rate is a market interest rate.

2.1.2. Currency swaps

A currency swap typically involves an initial exchange of currencies by the counterparties with an exchange in the opposite direction at the end of the swap. The counterparties might initially exchange JPY for USD, with one paying JPY and receiving USD while the other pays USD and receives JPY. At the maturity of the swap the counterparties exchange currencies in the opposite direction. In other words, the party that received USD at the initiation of the swap pays USD at the maturity of the swap. Each party's interim payments are based on the prevailing rates for the currency that it receives. So the swap coupon for the party that receives USD at the initiation of the swap is based on USD interest rates (because the USDs that are received could have been invested at these rates). Likewise, the swap coupon for the party that receives JPY is based on JPY interest rates.

To make currency swaps more concrete, suppose that firm A, which is located in Germany, would like to borrow USD to finance an investment in the US. The firm is well known in Germany, but not in the United States. It can borrow EUR for one-year at a fixed rate of 9% in Germany, but must pay 12% for USD in the U.S. Firm B would like to borrow EUR to finance an investment in Germany. This firm, which is well known in the U.S., but hardly known at all in Germany, can borrow USD at 10% in the U.S. and EUR at 13% in Germany. Both of these firms can reduce their cost of borrowing by executing a fixed-for-fixed currency swap. At the effective date of the swap, firm A borrows 10 million EUR in Germany and firm B borrows 5 million U.S. dollars in the U.S. The two firms then exchange currencies. At the maturity of the swap, firm A pays firm B 5.5 million USD and firm B pays firm A 10.9 million EUR. Each counterparty then has enough funds to pay off its loan. The cash flow for the combined swap and borrowings are as illustrated in Table 3.1. It might be worthwhile to note at this point that replacing each firm's direct borrowing with a swap exposes each firm to additional risks such as counterparty credit risk. Also, it is common to allow termination of a loan through early repayment, but swap agreements do not typically have provisions for voluntary early termination.

Table 3.1. Illustration of cash flows for a fixed for fixed currency swap

Action	Firm A Cash flow	Firm B Cash flow
At effective date of swap		
Borrows	+10 EUR	+5 USD
Exchange	-10 EUR for +5 USD	-5 USD for +10 EUR
At maturity		
Exchange	-5.5 USD for +10.9 EUR	+5.5 USD for -10.9 EUR
Repays	-10.9 EUR	-5.5 USD
Net cash flow	-0.5 USD	-0.9 USD
Cost of funds	0.5/5 = 10%	0.9/10 = 9%

In the case just illustrated, each firm has a comparative advantage in its home market. According to the **law of comparative advantage**, each country should specialize in producing the goods for which it has the lowest opportunity cost. It might be easier to understand the concept of comparative advantage by first examining product markets. Assume that the following conditions hold:

1. Country A can produce a toy truck using resources that cost 1 USD each and a hat at a cost of 1.5 USD each.[1]
2. Country B, on the other hand, produces a toy truck at a cost of 1.50 USD each and hats at a cost of 3 USD each.
3. Each country has 6 USD of resources.
4. Country A can produce 6 toy trucks or 4 hats, but given the preferences of its consumers it now produces 3 toy trucks and 2 hats.
5. Country B can produce 4 toy trucks or 2 hats, but given the preferences of its consumers, it now produces 2 toy trucks and 1 hat.

Hence, considering both countries together, currently, there is production and consumption of 5 toy trucks and 3 hats using 12 units of resources. In country A, in terms of resources, it costs (6/4 =) 1.5 toy trucks to produce a hat. In country B it costs (4/2 =) 2 toy trucks to produce one hat. In terms of a toy trucks, the cost of hats is higher in country B than in country A. Hence, country A has a comparative advantage in producing hats and country B has a comparative advantage in producing toy trucks.

If all the consumers in both countries purchase the 3 hats they currently consume from country A at a resource cost of 4.5, country A can also produce 1.5 toy trucks. Country B can then produce 4 toy trucks. In this case aggregate production and consumption would be 3 hats and (1.5 + 4) 5.5 toy trucks, which is 0.5 toy trucks larger than current consumption. When each country concentrates on producing the items for which it has a comparative advantage, aggregate production can be higher and, depending of the terms of trade, both countries can be better off.

---

[1] If you prefer not to have fractional units of production, you can assume that all monetary values and units of production are in millions.

2.1.3. *Commodity and equity swaps*

The Chase Manhattan Bank introduced commodity swaps in 1986 and these swaps rapidly became a standard product offered by many firms. One firm pays a fixed price to receive a floating price and the other firm pays a floating price to receive a fixed price. The floating reference price is often an average over some period rather than the price at a point in time. In a standard commodity swap, counterparties make payments based on the following formula:

Payment amount = ((Fixed price) X (no. of units of commodity Y))

– ((floating price) X (no. of units of commodity Z))

If the payment amount is positive, the firm agreeing to pay fixed makes the payment. Otherwise, the firm agreeing to pay floating makes the payment.

If Y and Z are the same commodity, as is usually the case, this formula becomes:

Payment amount = (Fixed-price – floating price)

X number of units of commodity

Consider an oil producer who wants to fix the price received for its oil over the next five years. When the oil is produced and sold on the spot market, the firm receives the current spot price. Hence, the goal of the firm is to swap the floating spot price received for a fixed price. The firm can accomplish its goal by entering into a swap in which it receives a payment if the floating price is less than a fixed price and makes a payment if the floating price is greater than a fixed price. If payments are received, they supplement the funds received from cash market sales. If payments are made, they offset funds received from cash market sales. These swap payments and receipts stabilize the cash flow.

In 1989, Banker's Trust developed equity swaps as an extension of commodity swaps. In an equity swap, one counterparty agrees to pay, and, the other agrees to receive the difference between a fixed rate and a floating rate. The primary difference between an equity swap and a commodity swap is that for the equity swap the floating rate is based on the total return (capital gain or loss plus dividends) on an index of equities. The index might be the Financial Times Index (London), the S & P 500, the Nikkei Index, or an index for a specific industry. A portfolio manager might use an equity swap to gain rapid exposure to the equity markets of a particular country or region.

There are many possibilities. A portfolio manager who owns U.S. stocks might swap the return on the S&P 500 for the return on the Nikkei Index, effectively converting an equity portfolio for one country into an equity portfolio of another. Further, the floating leg of a swap might call for the payment based on a weighted-average of the performance of a variety of indexes.

2.2. Beyond plain vanilla swaps

2.2.1. Variations in swap terms

Plain vanilla swaps can be tailored to meet the needs of a wide variety of clients. The possibilities are almost endless, but it may be useful to review a few examples. Several common variations involve changes in the amount of the notional principal over the life of the swap. **Amortizing swaps** provide for a decrease in the notional principal at one or more points during the tenor of the contract. For a special type of amortizing swap, the notional principal decreases in a manner consistent with the repayment of mortgages. **Accreting swaps** provide for an increase in the notional principal at one or more points during the tenor of the swap. A **roller coaster swap** allows for both increases and decreases in notional principal, following some pre-specified formula. In one formulation, payments by the floating ratepayer are added to, and receipts by the floating ratepayer are subtracted from, the notional amount.

Another common variation involves alternative specifications of the reset date. An average rate over a period is often used rather than a rate at a particular time. A bank relying on the overnight repo market to finance a project would likely encounter a different borrowing cost every day. A swap contract could be tied to the average of these rates.

A **par swap** in one for which the fixed and floating legs have about the same present value so that the net present value of the contract is zero. This is the most common case. Occasionally, a swap counterparty requires a swap coupon that is different from the current market price. Such a need might arise from a desire to match a specific cash market obligation. Swaps with a nonzero initial net present value are called **off-market**. An initial payment to bring the overall contract net present value to zero is then required. Of course, the net present value of a swap changes quickly after its creation as interest rates, currency exchange rates, and other factors that affect the obligations of the counterparties change.

In a basis swap a floating rate is exchanged for another floating rate, with each leg tied to a different index. The yield curve swap is also a floating-for-floating swap, but in this case each leg of the swap is tied to a different point on the yield curve. Floating-for-floating swaps are also typically available for currencies. As we have discussed in a previous chapter, there are LIBOR (London Interbank Offer Rates) quotes available for a number of currencies, including GBP, USD, and DEM. One or both legs of the swap could be tied to one of these rates. In another type of currency swap, there is no initial exchange of funds. Instead, the swap might call for one party to pay a fixed amount plus a fixed rate in DEM while the counterparty pays a fixed amount plus a floating USD LIBOR rate. This type of swap provides the DEM party with protection against changes in the USD exchange rate.

Zero coupon swaps have a fixed rate swap coupon that is zero. Hence, no payments are made on the fixed leg of the contract until maturity, when a single large payment is required. **Seasonal swaps** are designed to deseason a firm's cash flows. This can be accomplished in a variety of ways. One is to use a fixed-for-fixed swap with mismatched payment dates. Swaps that commence immediately, but for which the coupon rate is set later according to a procedure specified in the swap agreement are called **delayed-rate-setting swaps**. **Reversible swaps** call for the counterparties to switch roles as the fixed- and floating receiver.

2.2.2. Swaptions, caps, and floors

Swaptions are options on swaps. The holder of a swaption has the right to enter into a swap at a later date. Swaptions are useful if a firm may need a swap at a future date, but the need is not certain. The firm may have given a customer the option of purchasing its floating-rate debt at the end of six months. If the customer exercises its option, then the firm may want to convert the floating rate into a fixed rate using a swap. If the customer does not exercise the option, the firm will do nothing.

Floating rate obligations under a swap agreement can also be limited by the purchase of a cap or floor. A **cap** pre-specifies the maximum rate that will be paid and a **floor** places a limit on the minimum rate that will be paid. If the actual market rate is above the cap rate or below the floor rate, the holder of the cap or floor, respectively, receives a payment. Hence, caps and floors are similar to a multi-period call option and a floor is similar to a multi-period put option. On each reset date one option expires and the next begins. If the expiring option is in the money, the holder receives a payment. Otherwise, there is no payment on the cap or floor for that period. Caps and floors can be incorporated directly into swaps or purchased separately from a cap dealer.

A **collar** or **range forward** combines a long cap and a short floor. If on a given reset date the floating rate index is above the cap level the cap seller pay the cap buyer. If the index rate is below the floor level the floor seller pays the floor buyer. If the index level is equal to or between the cap and floor no payment is made. For example, a firm might enter into a range-forward swap on the price of gold with a cap of 310 USD and a floor of 250 USD. In this case, there would be no payments as long as the price of gold was in the range of 250-310 USD. But if the price exceeded 310 then one counterparty, say A, would be required to pay the other counterparty, say B. If the price fell below 250, then counterparty B would pay counterparty A. Notice that whether a cap or floor decreases or increases risk depends on which side of the agreement one is on. This is equivalent to options where the writer has unlimited risk (or nearly so) and the purchaser has limited risk. Through an appropriate selection of the cap and floor prices, a range forward swap can be initiated without the need for up front payments.

Participating forwards provide either a fixed cap and a flexible floor (which would be useful for a commodity user) or a fixed floor and a flexible cap (which would be useful for a commodity produce). In other words, one of the prices involved in the swap is fixed. For the fixed cap and flexible floor, the commodity user is compensated if the price of the commodity rises above the cap price. On the other hand, if the price falls below the cap price, the commodity user must pay an agreed upon percentage of the difference between the cap price and the market price to its counterparty. Like range forwards, if a suitable cap or floor rate is selected, participating forwards can be initiated without the need for any up-front payments.

3. The economics of swaps

Given that there are already numerous financial products available to firms, why has the market for swaps grown so rapidly? One reason is that financial objectives can often be accomplished quicker and easier and cheaper using swaps. Another reason for the widespread use of swaps is their usefulness in solving a wide variety of problems.

3.1. Advantages of swaps

Many capital market participants find swaps useful because, compared with alternatives, swaps can be implemented more quickly and cheaply.

Firms that are active participants in the swaps market can implement swaps almost immediately. The most important terms such as the tenor of the swap, the price and the reference rates can be negotiated, with the remaining details left for later. If both parties agree, the party on the side of the swap that is out-of-the-money can make a payment to the in-the-money party to terminate the swap. Even if a swap counterparty will not agree to terminate a swap another swap with offsetting obligations can often be initiated.

Swaps often have cost advantages over other strategies. The costs incurred in a swap may be less than the marketing and distribution costs, legal fees, rating agency fees, and similar costs of alternatives, especially if the alternatives involve the distribution or purchase of securities from the public. Taxes associated with the actual transfer of assets may be avoided. Further, swaps may provide an attractive vehicle for exploiting market inefficiencies.

3.2. Uses of swaps

Swaps can be used in a variety of ways. Swaps may provide a way to overcome lack of information about how particular markets operate, lack of experience in dealing in other markets and other barriers. It is well known that investors have a home country bias. In other words, investors prefer to invest in their home markets often even when the returns in nondomestic markets are higher. There are many obstacles to investing outside one's home country. A partial listing includes: lack of information about investment opportunities, lack of information about how the markets work and who can be trusted in these markets, and currency risks. If two firms can borrow more cheaply in their own countries than in each other's country, this inefficiency can be exploited so that each can potentially have lower borrowing costs.

Case: A company intends to finance a major acquisition using debt. When the acquisition agreement is signed, the company enters into a swap to lock in the current interest rate. As the negotiations proceed, if interest rates began to increase the company is protected. The rapidity with which swaps can be implemented is a critical factor in the choice of this strategy.

Case: In 1981, the World Bank, an international organization formally known as The International Bank for Reconstruction and Development, needed SFR and DEM to finance its operations in Switzerland and Germany. Salomon Brothers arranged a swap between the World Bank and International Business Machines in which the World Bank assumed SFR obligations of IBM and IBM assumed USD obligations of the World Bank. This swap allowed the World Bank to obtain the funds it needed without directly taping German or Swiss capital markets. The fact that two major institutions found it advantageous to use a swap to achieve their objectives provided early validity to the use of this strategy.

Firms that do not have credit ratings may find it difficult and costly to borrow.

Case: The subsidiaries of a major firm had difficulty borrowing at an acceptable fixed rate because of their lack of an independent credit rating. However, the subsidiaries found that they could borrow short-term at acceptable rates. Of course, because the borrowings were short term, the borrower paid a variable or floating interest rate. To convert these floating rate borrowings to fixed, the parent entered into a swap agreement with an outside counterparty. The agreement was down streamed to the subsidiary using a second swap between the parent and subsidiary. The firm felt that the combination of short-term debt with 100% backup through a revolving credit agreement combined with a swap was the equivalent of fixed-rate debt.

Swaps may provide a way of dealing with regulatory barriers. Many countries restrict portfolio investments by nondomestic investors. Swaps may provide a vehicle for gaining exposure to these markets. In addition, many countries place restrictions on the ownership of various types of assets. Firms may be able to gain exposure to the markets more easily using swaps than using actual assets. In other cases, swaps can be used to accomplish strategies that cannot be accomplished directly due to regulatory obstacles.

Case: An insurance broker collected premiums through agents. Government regulations required the collected funds (which typically amounted to $100 million) to be invested in Federal funds until they were received by the insurance broker. The broker wished to invest in longer-maturity instruments. A floating-for-fixed interest rate swap was an effect way of accomplishing this objective.

Investors may also face delays and high costs in altering their asset allocation. Swaps may allow asset allocations to be changed more quickly.

Case: An Australian pension fund holds a portfolio of U.S. stocks that tracks the S&P 500. The firm would like to convert its equity exposure to a fixed-rate exposure in AUD for a six-month period. This can be accomplished with a series of swaps. First, the fund swaps its equity return for a fixed UDS swap coupon. Next, the fund enters a fixed-for-floating interest rate swap tied to USD LIBOR. Finally, a floating-for-fixed currency swap into AUD completes the conversion of the fund's equity exposure into a fixed AUD exposure.

Firms that wish to make changes in their capital structure may find that selling or repurchasing equities and bonds cannot be accomplished quickly or cheaply. Swaps may provide a way of keeping the debt/equity ratio at a desired level between security issuance dates. Swaps can also be useful in managing individual debt and equity issues.

Firms commonly issue fixed-income debt that is non-callable for an initial period. Suppose that interest rates decline substantially during the call protection period. A firm might want to lock in these lower rates, but the existing debt must be dealt with first. One possibility is to repurchase the debt in the open market, but there is no guarantee that all of the debt can be repurchased and that the cost of repurchasing the debt will not wipe out the firm's gain from the fall in interest rates. Futures contracts with suitable length or timing of maturities are unlikely to be available. Swaps represent a practical alternative. In this case it is the flexibility of the swap contract that gives it an advantage. Here the firm can enter into a swap with a delayed starting date, which corresponds to the date on which the bonds can be called.

Swaps allow firms to accomplish changes in their inventories (including inventories of financial assets) without actually acquiring or disposing of the assets. Hence, long-established relationships with suppliers and customers that might be disrupted by other approaches are avoided through the use of swaps. The Phibro swaps described in Box 3-1 are typical. Since all of the swaps are settled in cash rather than through delivery, the client and vendor relationships of the swap counterparties are not affected. This approach might also avoid taxes that are triggered by an actual asset sale.

4. Valuation of swaps

At the initiation of a swap the net present value of the contract is zero. This is most often accomplished by setting both the fixed rate payment and the floating rate payment at market rates. If nonmarket rates are used, then a sufficient payment(s) must be made at some point during the life of the contract to restore the initial net present value to zero. Of course, after the commencement of the swap, changes in market interest rates will likely cause the swap to become an asset for one party and a liability for the other.

For most swaps semiannual payments are required. If the swap does not call for semiannual payments, market rates that are quoted on a semiannual basis must be adjusted. The general formula for converting payments compounded at one frequency per year into equivalent payments compounded at another frequency is

$$r_q = q \left((1 + r_z/z)^{z/q} - 1 \right)$$

where q and m indicate the number of compounding periods per year.

In order to aid in understanding swaps it may be useful at this point to consider the valuation of several swap contracts.

Case 1: A firm has issued 10,000,000 USD of bonds with five years to maturity with a fixed coupon of 8.65%. The firm approaches a dealer and seeks a quote for paying floating rather than fixed. The dealer looks at the five-year U.S. Treasury yield and offers to pay that rate plus 46 basis points,

---

Box 3-1. Illustrative strategies available to producers

and users of fuel oil

Crude oil and related products are essential to the operations of many firms, and, consequently, there are also many firms involved in their development and production. Phibro Energy, Inc. is a fully integrated trader of energy-related commodities and a leading provider of energy risk management. The following are four strategies Phibro suggests as being potentially useful to its clients.

Strategy 1: Operating hedge

An oil producer wishes to lock in a budget forecast for crude oil production for the next twelve months. The producer has budgeted 19 USD per barrel, a level at which the firm can conformably service its debt and earn an adequate profit margin. However, the firm wishes to achieve this objective while retaining some upside potential and avoiding premium payments. An average-price range forward collar with a twelve-month tenor may accomplish these objectives. The contract is based on the second nearby NYMEX light sweet crude oil contract. Settlement is in cash versus the average semiannual NYMEX close. The floor is 19 USD, the ceiling is 22 USD, and the premium is zero.

Using this swap, the producer can lock in a price range of 19-22 USD per barrel for designated amount of its production. Average semiannual second nearby NYMEX West Texas Intermediate (WTI) prices below the floor result in cash payments of the differential from Phibro to the producer, whereas average prices above the ceiling result in cash payments from the producer to Phibro. The producer has protected its budgeted oil price without up front premium, and has retained three USD per barrel of upside potential above the floor level. Because the hedge contract is for cash settlement, the producer sells its oil as it normally would on the spot market.

Strategy 2: Strategic hedge

The producer wishes to develop marginal producing properties but is hesitant to do so because of price uncertainty. Prices below 16 USD a barrel make the economics of the project unattractive, and therefore the producer seeks floor protection at that price. To fully subsidize the purchase of this floor for the five year expected producing life of the reserves, the producer is willing to forego prices above a certain level. A long-dated average price range forward with a tenor of five years may accomplish the producer's objectives. The basis is the second nearby NYMEX light sweet crude oil contract along with a floor of 16 USD and a cap of 23 USD. Settlement is in cash versus the average semiannual NYMEX close. The premium is zero.

Over each semiannual period, average second nearby NYMEX WTI prices below 16 USD result in cash settlements of the differential times the semiannual volume from Phibro to the producer. Average prices above 23 USD result in cash settlements from the producer to Phibro. Average prices within the range require no cash settlements. The producer has locked in the minimum return on marginal properties, while retaining an additional 7 USD per barrel upside potential, and paying no up front premium. The development of such reserves could improve the firm's balance sheet with no threat to margins. Moreover, the bank, which usually lends 50% of the NPV of such reserves at a base case price, may wish to increase its credit because of the reduced price uncertainty.

Strategy 3: Fixed prices crack spread

An oil refiner is contemplating a refinery expansion to meet rising demand for refined products. The refiner will need to finance the expansion largely with bank debt, and in an effort to secure attractive terms the producer may want to lock in its crack spread on a portion of the refinery's capacity of 50,000 barrels per day. The crack spread certainty will allow security in servicing the debt needed for the refinery expansion. The tenor of the swap is four years. The contract is based on the semiannual average Platt's mean U.S. Gulf Coast unleaded gasoline price minus the semiannual average NYMEX WTI first nearby contract price. Settlement is in cash. The premium is 0. Crack spreads below 3.50 USD per barrel require cash settlements of the differential from Phibro to the refiner, whereas spreads

above 3.50 require cash settlements of the differential from the refiner to
Phibro.

Strategy 4: Long hedge

A forest products company burns 1mm barrels a year of residual fuel oil
to run it mills. Its profits have been eroded recently by the sharp upward
move in oil prices. Rearing higher future prices, and an inability to fully pass
these additional costs through to its customers, the firm would like
protection for its exposure to cost changes in U.S. Gulf Coast 1% residual
fuel oil prices. The firm can consider an oil price swap at a price of 19 USD
with a tenor of five years. The basis of the swap is Platt's mean assessment
USGC 1% residual fuel oil (waterborne). The swap calls for semiannual
cash settlement versus average Platt's mean close. The premium is 0. At the
end of each semiannual period, average Platt's mean quotations are
compared to 19 USD. Prices above 19 USD require cash settlement of the
differential times the semiannual volume from Phibro to the company,
whereas prices below 19 USD necessitate cash settlements of the
differential from the company to Phibro. The company continues to
procure its physical fuel through normal channels. The cash settlements
offset higher or lower prices, locking the user in at the swap level.

Source: Phibro Energy, Inc. Reprinted by permission.

or 8.42%, in return for LIBOR. To calculate the firm's cost, first note that
the swap requires the following payments

Payment on current debt:	8.65%
Receipt from swap dealer:	-8.42%
Payment to swap dealer:	LIBOR

It appears that the firm's cost is LIBOR plus (8.65% - 8.42%) 0.23%. But
there are two additional features of bond and swap quotations that must be
taken into account. The fixed payment for a swap and the payments on
bonds are calculated using **bond equivalent yield differential** which is
calculated using either *actual days/365 days* or *30 days/360 days*. LIBOR is
quoted using **money market yield differential** based on *actual days/360
days*. The following formula equates money market yield differences (M)
and bond equivalent yield differences:

$$M = (360/365) \, B$$

For this example, B = 0.23%, so that

$$M = (360/365)B = (360/365)\ 0.23\% = 0.227\%.$$

Hence, the firm's cost is LIBOR + 0.227%

Case 2: A dealer is quoting interest rate swaps at 9.63% semiannual versus LIBOR flat for a five-year swap with a 10,000,000 notional value. A client would like to pay 9.5% fixed. This is an off-market rate. What adjustments in the cash flows are required?

2A: One approach is to adjust the LIBOR payments as well. First, convert the fixed reduction of (9.63% - 9.50%) to money market basis as follows:

$$M = (360/365)B = (360/365)(-0.13\%) = -0.128\%.$$

Hence, the required floating rate is LIBOR - 0.128%.

2B: Another approach is to calculate the lump sum payment required to compensate for the reduced fixed-rate payments. The formula is

$$PV = P\ ((1 - (1 + r/m)^{-nm})/(r/m))$$

where PV is the present value, P is the annuity, r is the yield, m is the number of periods per year, and n is the number of years or tenor.

For this case, the reduced payments are $(0.0013(10,000,000\ \text{USD}))/2 = 6,500\ \text{USD}$ semiannually, r = 8.42%, m = 2 and n = 5.

$$PV = 6,500\ \text{USD}\ ((1 - (1 + (0.0842/2))^{-10})/(0.0842/2)) = 52,174\ \text{USD}.$$

This is the payment by the fixed-rate payer that is required at the initiation of the contract. If the initial swap coupon has an off-market rate that is lower than the market rate, as in this case, the payment is called a **buy down**. If the initial swap coupon is above the market rate, the floating ratepayer will make a payment and this is called a **buy up**.

Case 3: Continuing case 2B, what payment is required, if any, to terminate this swap at the first reset date if dealers are quoting fixed 9.87% versus LIBOR flat. Note that interest rates have increased so that the fixed-rate payer now has a valuable contract. Assume that the first floating-rate coupon is 8.65%.

If the termination is between reset dates then the cash flows outlined here must be discounted to the termination date. In addition, if the LIBOR flat rate has changed the first floating interest payment will be different and the difference between this rate and the original rate for the period from the termination date to the reset date must be taken into account.

Obligation of the fixed rate payer	USD
Present value of semiannual payment $475,000 \times ((1 - (1 + 9.87/200)^{-9})/(9.87/200)) =$	3,386,009
Present value of terminal "payment" $(1 - (1 + 9.87/200)^{-9}) =$	6,482,115
Present value of fixed interest payment at first reset date	475,000
Total obligation	10,343,124
Obligation of the floating rate payer	
Present value of interest and terminal payment at LIBOR flat	10,000,000
Present value of semiannual payment at first reset date	432,500
Value of buy down	46,332
Total obligation	10,478,832
Net payment from floating rate payer to fixed rate payer	135,708

5. The creation and trading of swaps

When the swap market was in its infancy, each swap dealer wrote his or her own contract. The initial agreement to enter into the swap was consummated over the telephone by agreement on a few key points such as the tenor of the agreement, the swap coupon rate, the floating rate index and premium and similar matters. These were confirmed in writing on a confirmation. But the actual agreement might be signed some time later and dealt with a wide variety of issues, which were of less, immediate concern, but which might also be important. These included issues such as the definition of default and the terminal value of the swap in the event of default, the identification of the jurisdiction in which disputes would be resolved, and the like. Legal review of each of each swap contract resulted in substantial costs. As the market developed, it became clear that standardization was needed. In 1985 the International Swap Dealer's Association published its first code, *The Code of Standard Wording, Assumptions and Provisions for Swaps, 1985 Edition*. The British Bankers Association also developed its own documentation, the *British Bankers' Association Interest Rate Swaps*. The availability of these standard documents greatly facilitated the development of the swaps market.

As we have seen, after their initial development, the market for swaps grew rapidly. But in 1987 the trading of swaps in the U.S. stopped for several years due to regulatory uncertainty. To understand why, it is necessary to understand some of the history of the regulation of futures trading in the U.S. When trading in futures contracts began in Chicago, the contracts were for the actual delivery of agricultural commodities and the right to demand and make delivery was incorporated into every contract. This right could be terminated only by the agreement of both parties, which necessitated their entering into offsetting transactions on floor of the exchange.

Eventually, a number of unscrupulous individuals set up firms that took orders from the public, but did not execute the orders on the exchange. Instead, the firms, which did not have adequate capital, assumed the counterparty risk themselves, typically without informing the customer. This practice is called **bucketing** and, hence, the firms were called **bucket shops**. The firms happily collected money from their customers for the initial margins plus any gains due to the firm as a result of marking the contracts to market daily. Small gains due to customers were also happily paid. If customers held contracts giving them substantial gains, the firm would simply fold up their operations and declare bankruptcy. The same individuals would then reopen under a new name in a new location. These bucket shops were legal as long as the firms intended to perform on the contracts and but it was difficult to prove that a firm did not intend to deliver until it was too late for the customers to recover their money. To combat these practices, individual states passed laws outlawing bucket shops as a form of gambling.

Subsequently, some investors attacked the legality of futures exchanges using the bucket shop laws. In *Board of Trade v. Christie*, the Supreme Court of the U.S. ruled that the futures contracts were legal because of the intent to deliver rather than make cash settlement. This ruling placed the right to deliver at the center of the determination of whether a contract was legal or illegal.

In 1933 the U.S. Congress passed the Commodities Exchange Act giving the newly established Commodity Exchange Authority jurisdiction to regulate "transactions involving sale of a commodity for future delivery." In 1974 Congress changed the name of the regulatory authority to the Commodity Futures Trading Commission and expanded its jurisdiction. Trading of futures contracts off an exchange was declared illegal.

The development of the swaps market in the early 1980s raised a number of legal issues. Were swap dealers illegal bucket shops under state laws since the swaps were typically settled in cash? Alternately, were swaps illegal off-exchange futures contracts? In 1987, the CFTC, stated that swaps were futures and, therefore, illegal. The market for swaps in the U.S. was effectively closed down. After these actions created a firestorm, the CFTC backed down and decided to exempt swaps from its jurisdiction. Here, two problems were encountered. The first problem involved regulatory jurisdiction. Critics complained that the CFTC did not have the authority to exempt swaps from its jurisdiction because the CFTC did not have the authority to regulate swaps. Since most swaps do not contemplate delivery, they do not meet the definition of "transactions involving sale ... for future delivery." Further, equities, debt instruments, loans, and foreign exchange are not commodities, as stated in the legislation. Moreover, even if swaps were futures contracts involving commodities, trading off an exchange was never contemplated. The second problem was that if swaps were not under its jurisdiction, the CFTC did not have the authority to make regulations preempting state bucket shop laws.

The U.S. Congress remedied this situation in 1991 when it gave the CFTC explicit authority to exempt swaps from its regulation if they met the following criteria:

- exemption is in the public interest,

- the counterparties are institutions,
- the creditworthiness of the counterparties is a material consideration, and
- the agreements are not standardized and not traded through a centralized facility.

The requirement that creditworthiness be a material consideration prevented the use of clearinghouses for swaps. The requirement that the contracts not be standardized hampers the creation of an over-the-counter secondary market in swaps. These problems have been address by new legislation discussed in the next section.

6. Swaps risks

Parties to a swap face credit risk due to the possible default of their counterparty. Of course, at the initiation of the swap, when the swap is typically at the money, there is no credit risk. Further, credit risk is minimized by the fact that either no principal is exchanged or, as in the case of currency swaps, the principal exchanged is of comparable value.

To help mitigate the risk of swaps, the Dodd–Frank Wall Street Reform and Consumer Protection Act (Dodd-Frank), which became law on July 21, 2010, introduced major changes in the regulation of swaps. And the regulatory landscape is rapidly evolving as portions of the law are implemented.[1] The law requires that many swaps be cleared through exchanges or clearinghouses. A Swap Execution Facility has been established where certain swaps and be traded and settled.[2] Dodd-Frank establishes Derivatives Clearing Organizations (DCO) that meet CCFTC requirements to clear swaps.[3] Swaps that are not cleared through a DCO must be reported to a Swap Data Repository.

Swap dealers face sovereign risk, in that changes in laws and regulations in a particular country may affect the ability of counterparties in that country

---

[1]
http://en.wikipedia.org/wiki/Dodd%E2%80%93Frank_Wall_Street_Reform_and
_Consumer_Protection_Act

[2] http://en.wikipedia.org/wiki/Swap_Execution_Facility

[3] A list of DSOs can be found at
http://sirt.cftc.gov/sirt/sirt.aspx?Topic=ClearingOrganizations

to fulfill their swap obligations. Swap dealers may limit their exposure to swaps in a particular country.

Unlike typical swap users, swap dealers hold many swaps. The changes in the value of these swaps are not offset by changes in the value of the dealer's inventory of commodities and financial instruments. Hence, management of the risk of this swap portfolio requires special attention. The portfolio of swaps is called the **swap book.** When the market for swaps was just getting started, swap banks matched clients with offsetting needs. The necessity of identifying two counterparties with opposite needs was an obstacle to the growth of the swap market. As the market grew and the dealers became more sophisticated, swap dealers began to manage their swaps as a portfolio rather than individually. Hence, the dealer attempts to assess the exposure of the entire portfolio to risks such as those from interest rate changes, yield curve shifts, exchange rate changes, basis changes (between LIBOR and U.S. Treasury bills, between commercial paper and Federal funds, and the like).

The portfolio approach to hedging is called a **macrohedge**. In one such approach, to hedge the fixed side of the swap book, the swap dealer determines the cash flows that are due during coming period. The length of these periods, which are called **buckets**, is arbitrary. The dealer then derives a zero coupon yield curve for the swaps portfolio and for a U.S. Treasury note. These two yield curves are used to calculate the amount of the Treasury note needed to hedge the dealer's swap exposure.[1]

7. Summary

A swap is a contract evidenced by a single document in which two counterparties agree to exchange periodic payments. The contract commences on its effective date and ends on its maturity date. The basic

---

[1] This method is described fully in: Bansal, V.K., M.E. Ellis, and J.F. Marshall, 1993, The spot swaps yield curve: Derivation and use, in Advances in Futures and Options Research, vol. 6; and in Kapner, K.R. and M.E. Ellis, 1992, Swap yield curves: Par, spot, and forward and the pricing of short-dated swaps, in The Swaps Handbook: 1991-92 Supplement, J.F. Marshall and K.R. Kapner, eds.

version of a swap is referred to as plain vanilla. In a plain vanilla interest rate swap, one counterparty agrees to make payments based on a floating rate and the other makes payments at a fixed coupon rate. The payments are typically calculated with reference to a notional amount since actual principal is not usually exchanged at the beginning or end of the contract. At each payment date the floating rate payment and the fixed payment are compared and the party owing the largest payment pays the difference to the counterparty. The required floating rate payment is determined at each reset date.

In a plain vanilla currency swap, the counterparties swap exchange currencies at the effective date and at maturity. The rates used to calculate both legs of the intermediate payments may be fixed. In a plain vanilla commodity swap one counterparty pays a fixed price to receive a floating price and the other counterparty pays a floating price to receive a fixed price. The floating reference price is often an average over some period rather than the price at a point in time. Commodity swaps have been extended to include swaps with floating or coupon rates based on the prices of financial products such as the S&P 500.

The possibilities for modifying plain vanilla swaps are endless. One modification that is now common affects the way the floating rate is calculated (for example, using an average price over a period rather than an end-of-period-price). Other modification affect variables such as the way the notional principal is calculated and the timing of payments.

Options on swaps are called swaptions. The holder of a swaption has the right to enter into a swap at a later date. A cap can be used to establish a maximum rate to be paid on the floating rate of a swap and a floor can be used to establish the minimum rate that can be paid on a floating rate. A collar combines a long cap with a short call.

Swaps have been highly successful because they can be implemented speedily, permit cost savings due to avoidance of marketing, legal, and distribution costs, and provide a way to make investments that would otherwise not be possible due to regulatory limitations. Taxes may also be avoided. Swaps may also provide a way for commercial enterprises to alter their capital structure, for investment managers to alter their asset allocation, and protect against losses due to fluctuations in inventory prices, including inventories of physical and financial assets.

A swap dealer is a counterparty to most swaps. The largest swap dealers are commercial banks. Swap dealers hold swaps in their investment portfolio. Swap dealers manage the risk of their swap book in a number of ways. Use of master agreements limits risk of default affecting just contracts on which the defaulting party has losses. Firms may also limit their dealing with individual counterparties based on the creditworthiness of the counterparty. It is now common practice to manage the swap book using a macro-hedge or portfolio approach. Methodologies have been developed to help swap counterparties evaluate the risk they face given various changes in asset prices and market rates for interest, foreign exchange and the like.

Swap valuation is based on the net present value of the two legs of the swap. At the initiation of the swap, the net present value is zero. Subsequent movements of market interest rates or asset prices result in one counterparty having an asset with a positive value and the other counterparty having a liability.

Questions

1. Define the following: swap, actuals, notional assets, and value date.
2. What are the major categories of swaps? Explain briefly.
3. Give an example of a plain vanilla interest rate swap.
4. What is the main advantage of using currency swaps?
5. Is a swaption the same as a swap? Explain.
6. What kinds of variations are available on swap terms?
7. Explain the advantages of swaps.
8. The word bucket has two different meaning in this chapter. Explain each.
9. Explain the risks faced by swap participants?
10. How can a dealer hedge against swap exposure?

References

Brown, Brendan, 1989, The Economics of the Swap Market. London: Routledge.

Marshall, John F. and Kenneth R. Kapner, 1990, Understanding Swap Finance. Cincinnati, OH: Southwestern Publishing.

Marshall, John F. and Kenneth R. Kapner, 1993, Understanding Swaps. New York: Wiley.

McCord, James H. and Allan C. Martin, 1993, Derivatives--power tools for pension funds, Financial executive, November/December 1993.

Saber, Nasser, Interest Rate Swaps: Valuation, Trading and Processing. Irwin: New York.

CHAPTER FOUR

HEDGING

Key Terms

Basis—the difference between the cash price of an asset and its futures price.

Cross-hedge—the use of a futures contract on one asset to hedge price movements in another asset.

Currency overlay manager—a firm employed to actively and independently manage a portfolio's foreign exchange exposure with a view to reducing risk from this source.

Economic approach to hedge determination—a method of determining whether a short or long hedge is required by examining the gains and losses from the cash asset and the derivative position.

Gap management—the selection of assets and liabilities according to their duration to achieve a target hedge.

Hedge—an asset position whose payoffs are acquired to offset risk due to price fluctuations of other assets.

Hedge fund—an investment fund that (1) charges a management fee based on its overall performance, (2) increases exposure to unsystematic risk due to leverage, (3) minimizes exposure to systematic risk through short selling.

Hedge ratio—the number of derivative contracts that are needed to hedge a given natural position.

Hedging—the acquisition of financial contracts or real assets to reduce or eliminate risk.

Long hedge—a position in a financial instrument that benefits from an increase in the price of an asset.

Natural long—a cash position that suffers a loss from a decrease in the price of an asset.

Natural short—a cash position that suffers a loss from an increase in the price of an asset.

One-sided natural position—an ownership interest that benefits from price movements in one direction but is not affected by movements in the opposite direction.

Perfect hedge—a hedge position that completely eliminates risk due to fluctuations in the price of the hedged asset.

Short hedge—a position in a financial instrument that benefits from a decline in the price of an asset.

Speculation—the taking of positions in financial assets that are especially risky or short-term in nature, or entering into derivative contracts with the intention of profiting from price changes rather than using the gains to offset losses on other assets.

Speculator—a type of investor who engages in speculation.

Stress test—evaluating the value of a portfolio of derivatives by changing the assumption about economic and financial variables such as interest rates.

Substitute action approach to hedge determination—a method of determining whether a short or long hedge is required by examining the definition of a long and short hedge.

Two-sided natural position—an ownership interest that benefits from price movements in one direction, but losses from price movements in the opposite direction.

Value at risk—the monetary amount of the decline in value that a derivatives portfolio can be expected to sustain during a specified percentage of time periods.

IN THIS CHAPTER, we explore the concept of hedging and explain its economic role and the economic basis of hedging. We also explore how derivatives can be used to hedge.

This chapter is divided into two main sections. In the first, we provide the background necessary to understand hedging. Specifically, we

- define hedging and identify its economic purpose
- discuss types of inventory positions and how each can be hedged
- discuss how to ascertain what type of hedge is needed

Then, in the next section, we provide a detailed graphical and quantitative discussion of natural and derivative outcomes. We use graphs to explain the various considerations in hedging. Further, we consider hedging for various natural positions, using the following derivatives:

- long futures, short futures , buying calls, buying puts, writing calls, and writing puts.

1. Introduction

Business owners want to earn a profit by supplying products and services. Risk is inherent in all businesses and the expected profits must be sufficient to compensate investors for bearing these risks. Nevertheless, there may be some specific risks that investors in a particular business do not wish to bear. This is especially true if there is a small but real risk that a particular occurrence could have serious consequences and possibly even lead to the bankruptcy of the organization. Consider a firm that has a single manufacturing facility. If the plant were destroyed by fire, earthquake or by other causes the firm might be ruined. Consequently, businesses often purchase property insurance to allow the plant to be rebuilt and business interruption insurance to compensate for lost profits during the period the firm is out of business. If the likelihood of loss is very high, the insurance premium will be prohibitive. If the likelihood of loss is very small, insurance may not be necessary.

Similarly, firms may hold large inventories of an asset relative to their total assets. These inventory positions may be required as a part of the firm's business. For example, an underwriter may acquire a large bond issue that it indents to sell to investors. The firm may wish to transfer the risk due to possible fluctuations in the bond's price to others. This is called hedging.

2. Background and framework for understanding hedging
2.1. Hedging defined

Hedging is the acquisition of financial contracts or real assets to reduce or eliminate risk. In some cases, hedging programs that are supposed to reduce risk have resulted in the bankruptcy of firms because those running the programs did not clearly understand hedging. A key to understanding the nature of hedging is to understand what hedging is not. Hedging is not speculation; hedging is the opposite of speculation. In this book, we define **speculation** as the taking of positions in financial assets that are especially risky or short-term in nature, or entering into derivative contracts with the intention of profiting from price changes. Thus, while the goal of a hedger is to eliminate risk, the goal of a speculator is to make a profit by taking risk. A **speculator** is a type of investor.

Derivative instruments are the tools typically used in hedging. But as the definition of speculation makes clear, derivatives are also used for speculation. Indeed, the only way to distinguish whether a transaction is hedging or speculation is to know the motive of the initiator of the transaction. Hedging and speculation are often opposite sides of the same coin.

2.2. Economic purpose

Hedging serves real economic purposes and, in fact, can lower the risk faced by investment bankers in underwriting securities, lowering the cost of capital. Hedging can lower the risk faced by producers, lowering the cost of many types of products. Hedging can help financial institutions manage the risk profiles of their assets so that their level of risk is tailored to specific requirements. Because hedging is so useful, managers and investors need to understand hedging.

It is impossible to have hedging without speculation. Without speculators the hedging markets will not work. Therefore, it follows logically that speculation using derivatives also serves real economic purposes and contributes to reducing the costs of production. Individuals who attack speculation as an evil may lack an understanding of how risk management works. We return to these topics later in the chapter, but first we describe hedging.

Business of all kinds including manufacturers, retailers, farmers, and financial services are in business to make a profit by selling a product or service for more than its cost of production. Often, fluctuations in the prices of inventories of various types are large enough to threaten the financial viability of a firm. If firms hold large inventories or are committed to make purchases at a fixed price, they may suffer from a fall in price. Or if a firm is committed to deliver products at a fixed price and these products are not held in inventory, the firm may suffer a loss if the price of the product increases. The competitors of these firms may be new entrants or established firms without inventories. In either case they will not have suffered inventory losses. Hence, a firm that does have inventories will not be able to pass these losses on to its customers. Therefore, firms frequently seek to protect themselves from changes in the prices of inventories. This protection is called a **hedge**. A **perfect hedge** completely eliminates risk due to fluctuations in the price of the hedged asset.

Why would anyone want a perfect hedge? Hedgers may give up potential gains from their positions in assets to protect themselves from losses. Some individuals and firms seek to profit from inventory price fluctuations. In other words, they speculate. But we think that it is best to view speculation as a separate activity from a firm's normal business. Why would an oil company drill for oil, and build refineries and distribution networks if its goal was to speculate on the price of oil? It would be far simpler to speculate on oil prices using financial instruments and derivatives. Then all the firm needs is a trader, capital, and electronic connections to brokers. Why would a farmer labor in the hot sun all day in order to speculate on the price of a crop? Of the farmer would not do this. The goal of producers is to sell their products at a price that covers the costs of their inputs and leaves a profit. In the case of the farmer, these costs include seeds, fertilizer, land and buildings, equipment, farm labor, taxes, and interest. If the farmer can make money by predicting price movements, there would be no need to own a farm. The farmer could make much more money much more easily simply by becoming a speculator. Businesses want to make money from their operations, not from inventory profits or speculation.

Hedging is not free. There are transaction costs. Moreover, if speculators demand compensation for absorbing the net supply of hedgers, the speculators will earn this compensation from the hedgers on the side of the market most in demand. The risks faced by a business due to inventory fluctuations must be significant for it to be worthwhile to incur hedging costs. If fluctuations in inventory prices could lead to financial distress resulting in, say, the downgrading of a firm's credit rating or even bankruptcy, hedging is likely justified. A stable earnings stream may attract better employees and protect managers' jobs. If the firm's stockholders hold undiversified portfolios, it may be more cost effective for the firm to hedge than for the stockholders to hedge.

The essence of investing is risk-taking. Clearly, investors may find hedging useful for making temporary alterations in their portfolios. Whether other types of hedging make sense for investors is an open question. International investors face both investment risk and exchange rate risk. Moreover, the exchange rate risk is typically greater, resulting in more return variability, than the investment risk. Some argue that this risk should be hedged and others argue that it should not be hedged. We explore the reasons for the contradictory views later.

2.3. Natural longs and shorts

2.3.1. Natural longs

Many individuals and firms own raw materials and other inventory that they plan to use in producing products. Refineries own inventories of crude oil, which may be in storage tanks on site or in large ocean-going tankers in transit from distant oil fields. Manufacturers of food products hold large inventories of agricultural commodities such as wheat, soybeans, and corn. Meat packers own cattle and hogs. Industrial metals such as copper used in manufacturing electronic goods may be held in inventory. Jewelry and photography film manufacturers, among others, hold inventories of precious metals such as gold and silver. All of these manufacturers are natural longs. A **natural long** suffers a loss from a decrease in the price of an item used in the course of their business. A natural long may, but does not necessarily, benefit from an increase in the price of the inventory.

Not all natural longs are involved in manufacturing. Banks hold large positions in fixed income and equity securities. If the prices of these financial instruments go up, the banks are better off. But if the prices decline, the banks incur are worse off. Thus, banks are natural longs with respect to this part of their portfolio. Pension plans, insurance companies, and individual investors also own large positions in fixed income securities and in stocks. They too are natural longs.

Of course, natural longs are happy to benefit from price increases. The problem is that while there may be gains if prices increase there may be losses if prices decline. If these losses are sufficiently large, they can lead to the bankruptcy of a business. Probably the best example of the problems that can be encountered by natural longs is the widespread bankruptcies of savings and loan associations in the U.S. during the 1980's. It is well known that increases in interest rates cause prices of fixed-income securities to fall and that decreases in interest rates cause prices of fixed-income securities to rise. In general, the longer the duration of the instrument the greater its price change in response to a given interest rate movement. Savings and loans borrowed funds in the form of deposits from their customers. These deposits, which represented liabilities of the savings and loans, were typically repayable in full at face value on demand. For many years, the rates U.S. savings and loans could pay depositors were fixed by U.S. government regulation. In the early 1980s interest rates increased dramatically. The difference between what savings and loans were allowed to pay depositors and market interest rates became so great that investors began to make enormous withdrawals from savings and loans. To prevent these outflows the government was forced to remove restrictions on the interest rates these institutions could pay depositors. Since the deposits were essentially cash equivalents, these liabilities did not fluctuate in value with changes in market interest rates. So the increase in interest rates did not affect the value of the liabilities of savings and loans, but did increase their costs of funds.

The savings and loans used their deposits to invest primarily in mortgages on residential and commercial real estate. Mortgages are long-term financial instruments. When deposit interest rates were fixed, the rates that savings and loans earned on the mortgages were higher than the rate paid to depositors so that after expenses most savings and loans earned a profit. With respect to their holdings of mortgages, the savings and loans were natural longs. When interest rates increased the value of the mortgages declined. In many cases, the value of the assets fell below the obligations owed to depositors and the savings and loan became insolvent. The U.S. government insured most of these institutions through the Federal Savings and Loan Insurance Corporation. Hence, the U.S. government came to own a large part of the savings and loan industry which required a number of years to liquidate.

2.3.2. Natural shorts

Just as there are businesses that are natural longs, there are also businesses that are natural shorts. A **natural short** gains from a decrease in the price of an item used in the course of its business. A natural short may, but does not necessarily, suffer losses from an increase in the price of the item. For manufacturers, being a natural short means that the business has a negative inventory. In other words, the business has agreed to sell its products at a fixed price, but does not own the materials needed to manufacture these goods or does not have the item in stock. These products may incorporate large amounts of raw materials. Hence, in effect, the firm has negative inventory. An insurance company may have sold an insurance contract that calls for the policyholder to pay a premium of 50,000 USD in six months. If the insurance company has guaranteed a fixed rate of interest to the policy holder and interest rates fall, the policy holder will be better off, but the insurance company will be worse off. Note that the fall in interest rates results in an increase in the value of the policy. Thus, the insurance company is a natural short.

2.4. Two-sided versus one-sided positions

Both two-sided and one-sided natural positions can arise from a firm's inventory positions. Two-sided natural longs benefit from an increase in the price of an item used in its business, but also suffer losses from a decrease in the price of the item. Likewise, a two-sided natural short benefits from a decrease in the price of an inventory item, but suffers losses from an increase in the price of the item. In contrast, one-sided natural longs or shorts face risk if the price moves unfavorably, but do not benefit from a favorable price move. The definitions of long and short used here allow for both one-sided and two-sided outcomes by ignoring price changes that are favorable. Protection is needed only for the unfavorable outcomes. One-sided natural positions most commonly arise out of contractual relationships such as those between firms and their suppliers or customers.

An investor who owns a portfolio of common stocks has a two-sided natural long position. The investor benefits from an increase in the price of the stocks and suffers from a decline in the price of the stocks.

An oil exploration and production company may have agreed to deliver oil to a refinery under a firm contract at a fixed price over the next five years. If the price of oil increases the production company is worse off, but is better off if the price of oil declines. The producer has a two-sided natural short and the refinery has a two-sided natural long.

Figure 4.1 shows the payoff profiles for two-sided natural longs and shorts. The current price of the asset is 5. Price decreases produce losses for the natural long and price increases produce losses for the natural short. These are the changes in inventory values that firms and individuals may wish to avoid.

A farmer often has a one-sided natural long position. Consider a Florida farmer with orchards of orange trees. A decrease in the price of oranges harms the farmer. If prices increase, the farmer may or may not benefit. The outcome depends on the reason that prices increase. If a freeze destroys the orange crop in Brazil, the farmer will benefit from the higher prices. But instead, if the freeze is in Florida the farmer may not benefit if the freeze has destroyed his crop. Thus, the farmer has a one-sided natural position. It is also important to specify which side requires the hedge. In the farmer's case, a one-sided hedge with protection from a price decline is needed.

As part of the sale of a fleet of cars a manufacturer agrees to reimburse the client for any increase in the price of oil during the next 30 days. If the price of oil increases the manufacturer will lose. But if the price of oil declines, the manufacturer will be in exactly the same position as at the start

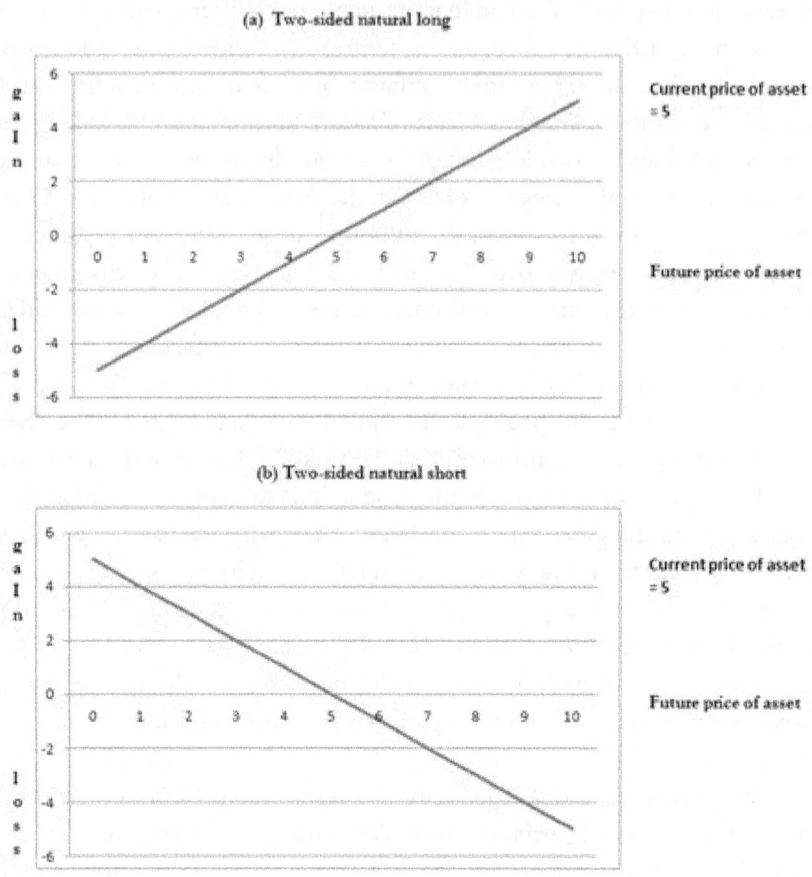

Figure 4.1. Profiles of outcomes for two-sided natural positions.

of the 30-day period. The manufacturer has a one-sided natural short position.

The payoff outcomes for the one-sided long and short natural positions are presented in Figure 4.2. Prices can either increase or decrease. We are only concerned with a price increase that produces a loss or a price decrease that produces a loss. Hence, there are two possible one-sided price profiles.

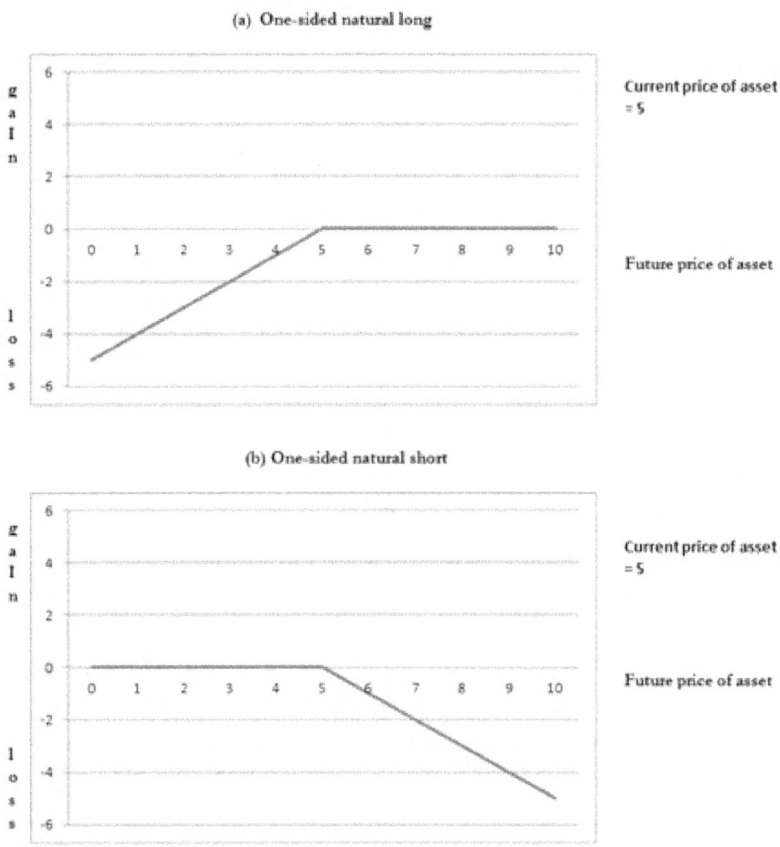

Figure 4.2. Profiles of outcomes for one-sided natural positions.

2.5. Long and short hedges

There are two types of hedges: long hedges and short hedges. To understand hedging one must understand each and be able to recognize when each is appropriate. We have seen that there are natural longs and natural shorts. The position that is required to hedge a natural long is called a short hedge. The position that is required to hedge a natural short is called a long hedge. Knowing that short hedges go with natural long positions and that long hedges go with natural short positions minimizes potential confusion resulting from terminology.

A **long hedge** is a position that benefits from an increase in the price of an asset. Likewise, a **short hedge** is a position that benefits from a decline in the price of an asset. A natural long incurs losses from a price decline; hence, to offset these losses a short hedge is needed. A natural short experiences losses from a price increase; hence, to offset these losses a long hedge is needed. We elaborate on these ideas below.

2.6. Determining the type of hedge needed

There are two basic ways of determining whether a short hedge or a long hedge is needed in a particular circumstance. We consider each.

2.6.1. The economic approach to hedge determination

One way is to look at the gain and loss profile of the natural position and to take a derivative position that provides protection from risk of loss. We call this the **economic approach to hedge determination**. Assume that the goal of the hedger is to completely eliminate risk due to price fluctuations in the natural position. Then, to provide a hedge, a derivative must provide a gain when the natural position has a loss. If the goal of a hedger is to completely eliminate risk, obtaining a perfect hedge, the monetary value of losses in the hedge position must exactly match the monetary value of gains from the natural position. If the natural position is two-sided, then it may be cheaper to allow losses on the hedge position to offset gains on the natural position. In these cases the hedger gives up the potential for gains in return for the protection afforded by the hedge. The hedger may be willing to give up these potential gains to save money on the cost of obtaining the protection of the hedge and because the firm is not in the business of speculating on price changes on inventory assets.

2.6.2. The substitute action approach to hedge determination

Alternatively, one can use the **substitute action** approach by deciding what action with respect to the natural position is required to eliminate the price risk. In other words, a firm with a natural long position in an inventory item can eliminate its price risk by selling the inventory. If selling the actual inventory is not desirable or practical, the sale can be replicated using a derivative instrument. Thus, a financial position that locks in a sale price provides a short hedge. Similarly, if a natural short purchased an offsetting position in the asset, price risk would be eliminated. Again, replicating the purchase with a derivative instrument provides a hedge. We call this the substitute action approach.

The substitute action approach is simplest to understand for futures, but also works for options. The following definitions from the CBOT spell out the substitute action approach for futures:

- The short hedge is, in essence, the sale of a futures contract as a substitute for the sale of the actual commodity.
- The long hedge is, in essence, the purchase of a futures contract as a substitute for the purchase of the actual commodity (CBOT, n.d.).

These definitions are specifically for futures contracts. But once the appropriate type of hedge is determined, a decision can be made on whether to use futures, options or swaps.

Risk of price changes from natural long positions can be eliminated by buying or selling the asset (depending on whether one is a natural long or short) or by a long or short hedge. In other words, selling a futures contract as a substitute for selling the actual asset can eliminate the inventory risk. Why not just sell the underlying interest? Often it is not available for sale. A farmer may not be able to sell a crop that is still growing in the field. Oil in transit has not yet arrived at the refinery. Premiums to be invested may not have been received from policyholders. A building to be financed with permanent funds may not have been fully built. Futures and options can be used to lock in purchase and sales prices without regard to the availability of the actual inventory.

For identifying hedge types, the CBOT definitions are typically easier to apply than the economic outcome approach. When applied to options, the CBOT definitions provide an indication of which option positions are likely to provide the most effective hedges. Since a put locks in a sales price, it is likely to provide the best hedge for a natural long position. And since a call locks in a purchase price, the call is likely to provide the best hedge for a natural short position. In some cases the economic approach is easier to use. Naturally, when used correctly, our two approaches give the same answer concerning the required hedge.

2.6.3. Problems with obtaining a perfect hedge using futures

We assume that in most cases the goal should be to obtain a perfect hedge. Deviating from this goal makes one a speculator subject to all of the risk associated with speculation. If the goal is to completely eliminate risk, the monetary value of gains in the hedge position must exactly match the monetary value of losses from the natural position.

There are a number of potential obstacles that may prevent a perfect hedge being achieved. We defined basis as the difference between a cash price and a futures price or between two futures prices. We also indicated some reasons that basis might change over the life of a futures contract such as changes in the availability of transportation. Changes in basis affect the ability to achieve a perfect hedge. We examine additional problems in obtaining a perfect hedge in the remainder of this section.

Maturity mismatch An importer may need to buy JPY in 6 weeks to make a payment for purchases, but the futures contracts available for hedging may have maturities of 4 weeks or 8 weeks.

Contract size mismatch Also, the there might be a mismatch between the amount of currency covered by the futures contract and the amount that the importer needs.

Cross-hedge There may not be a derivative with an underlying asset that matches the hedger's needs. A **cross-hedge** is the use of a futures contract on one asset to hedge price movements in another asset. An investment banker might use the CBOT U.S. Treasury bond contract to hedge a cash long position in corporate bonds since there are no futures contracts on individual corporate bonds. In general, interest rate movements will cause the prices of the corporate bonds and the U.S. Treasury bonds to move together. But there might be differences. For example, changes in the rate of taxation of corporate bonds relative to government bonds could cause differential price changes in the two types of bonds.

2.7. Potential problems with hedging programs

The purpose of hedging is to eliminate risk. But managers need to be careful about how hedging programs are implemented. There are numerous examples of firms that have started hedging programs that subsequently began speculating. Sometimes rogue employees subvert the hedging program. Or managers may decide that they a prescient about future prices.

Problems with hedging programs are not limited to rogue employees or managers who decide they can predict future prices. One of the largest derivative losses of all time came about through an apparent failure of senior management to understand the nature of hedging. MG Refining and Marketing (MGRM) was the U.S. subsidiary of the German firm, Metallgesellschaft AG (MAG), a conglomerate with more than 250 subsidiaries in the fields of trade, engineering, and financial services. MGMR operated a hedging program that began to require substantial cash flow to cover margin losses on the futures positions used to hedge the firm's natural long position. Reacting to the increasing cash flow requirements, senior management in Germany fired the US management team and installed a new management team for MRMG. The new management liquidated the hedge, which eventually resulted in a loss of 1.3 billion USD on the exposed natural position. Additional details are provided in Box 4.1.

Box 4.1. Metallgesellschaft AG

Metallgesellschaft AG (MAG) illustrates the risks of hedging programs.

During the early 1990s MAG, whose major stockholders included several German banks, owned more than 250 subsidiaries operating in such diverse activities as trading, engineering, and financial services. One MGA's subsidiaries, the U.S. firm MG Refining and Marketing (MGRM), sold and stored petroleum products. MGMR entered into five-year, fixed-price contracts with its customers on heating oil, gasoline, and diesel fuel. Customers were allowed to terminate their contracts if market prices increased significantly above the MGMR contract price. MGMR wanted to profit from its marketing and storage expertise, but did not want to speculate on oil price fluctuations.

MGMR's natural position was short so to hedge the firm entered into long crude oil contracts traded on the New York Mercantile Exchange. Because of their liquidity, the firm mostly used contracts with a one-month maturity, rolling over the contracts as they matured. MRMG went long sufficient contracts to offset its entire natural short position.

Futures prices equal the current spot price plus the basis. If the basis is positive the market is in contango and if the basis is negative the market is in backwardation.

For a physical commodity, basis reflects physical storage costs (warehouse space) and interest costs, less any benefit (convenience yield) from having inventory on hand to prevent stock outs. Futures markets for most physical commodities are typically in contango, but when MGMR initiated its hedging program and continuing for several years thereafter the crude oil futures market was in backwardation. Consequently, each time the futures contracts expired there was a gain.

In 1993 crude oil prices fell dramatically, causing losses on the futures leg of MGMR's hedge. Moreover, the market moved to contango. MGMR experienced a gain on its natural position that more than offset its loss on its futures position (assuming that its customers did not default), but there was a cash flow problem because the futures contract was marked to market daily, requiring significant additional margin, while the futures position was not marked to market until delivery. MGMR quickly exhausted a 500 million USD line of credit. Moreover, the New York Mercantile Exchange asked for additional margin above that normally required.

At first MGMR's parent met its needs for funds to meet its margin requirements, but as the demand for funds grew, the parent became alarmed and brought in new management for the subsidiary. The new management team liquidated the hedging program. Termination of the hedging program left MGMR unhedged and subsequent oil price increases resulted in losses of 1.3 billion USD. Culp and Miller (1995) characterize this as evidence of operational risk in that it reflects a failure of the parent's board to understand that MGMR was hedging and not speculating.

Note: For a discussion of using short-term futures contracts to hedge longer-term cash positions see: Culp, Christopher L. and Merton H. Miller, 1994, Hedging a flow of commodity derivatives with futures: Lessons from Metallgesellschaft, Derivatives Review 1; and Culp, Christopher L. and Merton H. Miller, 1995, Journal of Applied Corporate Finance 7, 62-76.

Risks of hedging programs such as those faced by MGMR must be recognized by management. Managers need to **stress test** their hedges by examining the outcomes if the assumptions made in initiating the hedge prove to be incorrect. Moreover, managers need to consider both usual and worse case departures from expectations. Failure to adequately consider these worse case scenarios is one of the main reasons that hedging programs fail.

3. Hedging with futures and options contracts

In this section we deal with hedging using futures contracts and options contracts, but not with swaps or forward contracts, which are over-the-counter alternatives. The concepts presented here for futures and options also generally apply to all derivatives. It may be possible to initiate the options strategies examined here using either exchange-traded or over-the-counter options.

3.1. Hedging two-sided natural positions with futures

Figure 4.3 shows the profiles of possible outcomes at maturity for long and short futures contracts. The value of the underlying asset is presented on the horizontal axis and the monetary outcome is presented on the vertical axis. Price increases are potentially unlimited. Hence, considering price increases, the potential gain for a long futures and the potential loss for a short futures are unlimited. Because price decreases are bounded by 0, the potential losses on long futures and gains on short futures are also bounded. However, practically we can also view the gains or losses from a price decrease as unlimited.

Combining the two-sided natural long position shown in Figure 4.1 (a) with the short futures position shown in Figure 4.3 (b) eliminates gains and losses from changes in the asset value. Similarly, combining the natural short position shown in Figure 4.1 (b) with the long futures position shown in Figure 4.3 (a) also eliminates gains and losses from changes in the asset value. In this case we have produced a perfect hedge by completely eliminating risk due to fluctuations in inventory prices.

Note that in both of these cases we are able to use a two-sided hedge position because the natural position is two-sided. Essentially, we are paying

Note: contract price = intersection of the lines with horizontal axis

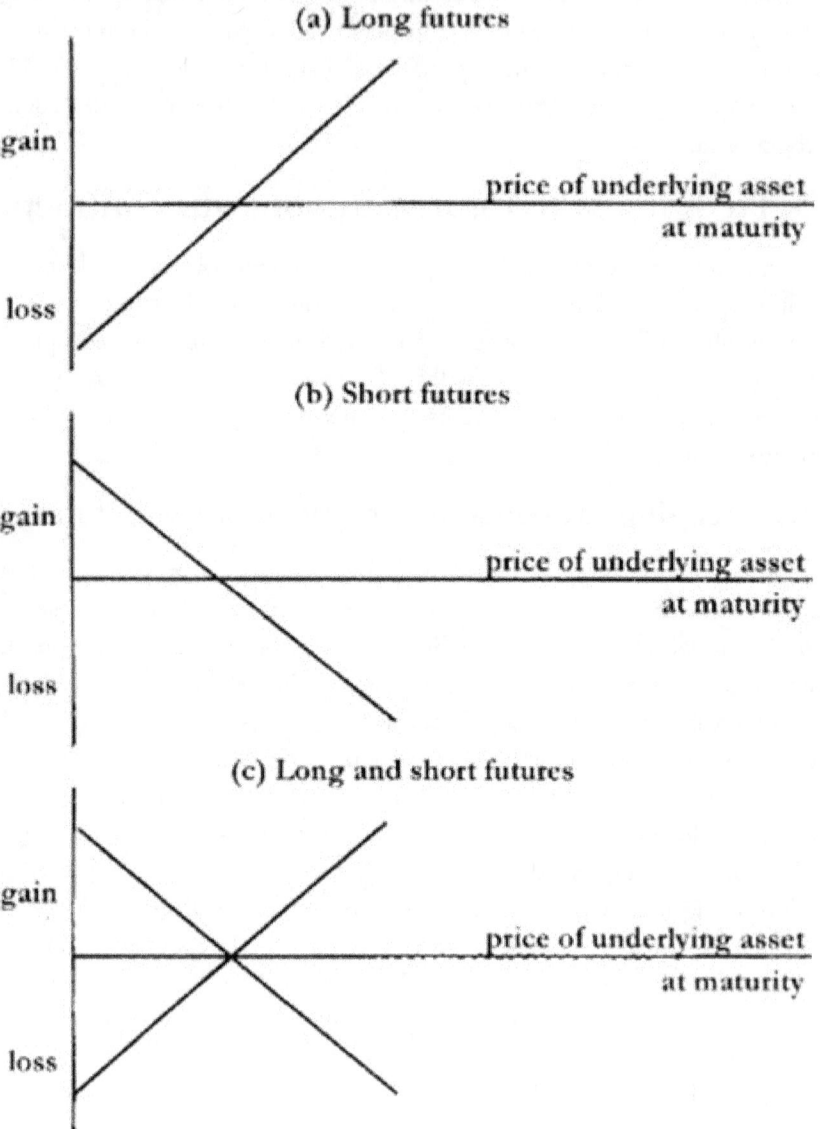

Figure 4.3. Profile of futures contract outcomes

for the loss protection by giving up the potential for gain from a favorable price movement.

3.2. Hedging with options

Now we consider using options as hedges. We use the terminology of writing an option and shorting an option interchangeably. Keep in mind that in hedging the goal is to eliminate risk of loss due to a price change in the natural position.

3.2.1. Case 1: Premiums = minimum value of the option, and the contract is at the money when hedge begins

To simplify the analysis, initially we assume that (1) the premium is equal to the minimum value of the option, and (2) the price of the underlying interest equals the striking price of the option at the initiation of the hedge. Note that when premiums are zero short option positions can produce only losses. Hence, the only two option positions that can be use in hedging are buying calls and buying puts. Clearly, a long natural position is hedged by buying a put and a short natural position is hedged by buying a call. Also, in this case no one would use futures contracts to hedge because with option premiums equal only to the minimum value of the options there would be nothing to lose by buying options to hedge. Clearly, this case is not realistic.

For one-sided natural positions, buying a put would hedge a one-sided natural long and buying a call would hedge a one-sided natural short.

3.2.2. Case 2: Hedging by buying options when excess premiums are positive

Next, we drop the assumption that option premiums are equal to the minimum value of the option, but retain the assumption that the price of the underlying security equals the striking price when the hedge is initiated.

First, we focus on **buying options for protection**. Just as in the previous case, clearly a natural long is hedged by buying a put and a natural short is hedged by buying a call.

However, now the hedge is not free—the hedger incurs the cost of the premium. Moreover, the greater the excess of the premium over the minimum value of the option the greater the cost. For one-sided natural positions, the cost of the premium must be weighed against the potential loss from the natural position just as one would do for an insurance policy.

For a two-sided natural position, if the expected value of the potential for gain from a favorable price movement is greater than the premium, then use of an option is indicated. Otherwise, it would be cheaper to use a futures contract. Suppose that an investor has a long position in the stock of IBM. This is a two-sided natural long that can be hedged by buying a put. If the price of IBM falls, the put will provide protection, but the protection will be reduced by the amount of the premium. If the price of IBM remains the same, the entire premium will be lost. If the price of IBM increases, the hedger will retain all of the increase in value of the IBM, but the gain will be reduced by the amount of the premium.

The most important difference in potential hedging strategies for case 2 is that under these assumption short put and call positions can produce gains. Hence, we need to consider **shorting options as hedges**. If the hedger writes and option and the option expires at the money or out of the money, the hedger gains the amount of the premium. This premium inflow can be used to partially hedge the natural position. This strategy is especially useful if the hedger expects only small changes in the price of the underlying asset. However, the hedger retains risk from large price movements in the underlying asset.

3.2.3. Case 3: Hedging with in-the-money and out-of-the-money options

Now we drop all our limiting assumption and examine the use of out-of-the-money and in-the-money options for hedging. For simplicity, we assume that the hedges are held until the expiration of the options. An out-of-the-money option can be purchased for a lower premium so that less money is at risk. On the other hand, an out-of-the-money option does not provide any hedge protection for the difference between the price of the underlying asset when the hedge is initiated and the strike price of the option.

If a hedge is obtained by writing options, the protection is provided by the premium received. Hence, options that are out-of-the-money provide less protection than in-the-money-options. On the other hand, options that are in-the-money have more premium at risk. At the expiration of the option, the writer must pay the amount that the option is in the money. If an out-of-the-money call has been written, the price of the underlying asset can increase up to the strike price before any money will be due at maturity. The writer of an in-the-money call receives a higher premium, but suffers from any increase in the price of the underlying asset. Writing puts as hedges works similarly. The hedger must evaluate the tradeoff between added protection and added risk.

Suppose that an investor owns a share of stock with a market price of 17 USD. Buying a put with a strike price of 15 USD provides protection for a drop below 15 USD, but not from a price decline from 17 USD to 15 USD. On the other hand, buying a put with a strike price of 20 USD provides complete protection, but incurs a much larger premium because this option is already 3 USD in-the-money.

An additional example might be useful. Suppose that the strike price for a call is 10 USD, the price of the underlying stock is 20 USD and the premium is 10 USD. You own 1 share of this stock that you wish to hedge. You write an option and receive 10 USD. At maturity if the price of the stock is 30 USD you repurchase the option for 20 USD. Your loss of 10 USD on the option is offset by the gain of 10 USD on the stock. However, if the price of the stock falls to 10 USD the option is worthless and you pocket the 10 USD that you received in premium. But you have lost 10 USD on the stock. In both cases you have eliminated your risk. However, if the price of the stock falls below the 10 USD strike price, you will have a loss on your natural position.

A short position in IBM can be hedged by buying a call or by writing a put. If the alternative of writing a put is chosen, then the amount of protection afforded is limited to the premium received. However, the investor also gives up the potential for gain if the price of the stock declines below the strike price. Suppose that the hedger can choose to hedge by buying an at the money call or writing an at the money put. If there is no change in the price of the underlying asset at maturity, the hedger would incur the premium as a cost in the first case and earn the premium in the second case. It is clear that hedgers need to carefully weigh various strategies.

3.3. Hedging with securities

Consider the U.S. savings and loans discussed earlier. As mentioned these savings and loans are natural longs with respect to their portfolios of mortgages. Therefore, a short hedge is required. The deposits of the savings and loans do not serve as a hedge because the value of these deposits generally does not fluctuate. We have examined the use of derivatives in establishing a hedge for the savings and loan. It is also possible to hedge using other types of securities. Of course, the savings and loan would be hedged if it simply sold its mortgages and held short-term instruments such as commercial paper with a one-day maturity. Based on the substitute action approach, it is clear that if the sale of the mortgages would eliminate price risk, a suitable hedge must provide the same type of protection. An alternative to using derivatives to hedge would be for the savings and loan to raise funds by issuing long-term bonds or long-term certificates of deposit. These securities might provide an effective hedge since their prices fluctuate in the appropriate direction when interest rates change.

Banks are major dealers in derivatives markets. In the course of their operations, they may find themselves with natural short positions in fixed-income obligations. One approach is to hedge these price risks with additional derivative contracts. But the bank might also be able to hedge by buying fixed-income securities.

3.4. Hedge ratios

There are at least three approaches used to determine the appropriate **hedge ratio**, the number of contracts that are needed to hedge a given natural position. One is the historical approach in which a historical relationship between the price changes of the futures contract prices and the price changes of the cash market are used to estimate a hedge ratio. Another uses the theoretical models to derive hedge ratios.

3.4.1. Historical data approach

In the historical approach, past price relationships are estimated and used to calculate hedge ratios. Suppose that we wish to use a futures contract on a cash commodity to hedge a natural position. We can derive the formula for the minimum risk hedge ratio. Let σ_F be the variance of the futures price, σ_s be the variance of the spot price, σ_{Fs} be the covariance of the prices of the futures and spot contracts and ρ_{sF} be the coefficient of correlation between the cash price and the futures price. We know that the variance of a portfolio (P) of one unit of the cash asset (s) and X units of the futures contract (F) is:

$$\sigma_P^2 = \sigma_s^2 + X^2\sigma_F^2 + 2X \, \rho_{sF} \, \sigma_s \, \sigma_F$$

Taking the derivative of portfolio risk with respect to X gives the following hedge ratio:

$$\text{Hedge ratio} = (\rho_{sF} \, \sigma_s \, \sigma_F)/\sigma_F^2 = \sigma_{sF}/\sigma_F^2 \text{ or } (\rho_{sF} \, \sigma_s)/\sigma_F$$

One way to estimate this hedge ratio is to regress the historical spot price holding period returns (R_s) on the historical futures holding period returns (R_f):

$$R_s = \alpha + \beta \, R_f + \varepsilon$$

where α and β are parameters to be estimates and ε is a random error term. The estimate of β is the risk-minimizing hedge.

In some cases we may have more than one spot price to deal with. Suppose that a bakery uses flour to produce bread. We are concerned about the price of the futures contract and two commodity prices, the price of flour and the price of bread. Assume that both the flour and bread are quoted in one unit, which we can define in any way we wish as long as we use the appropriate corresponding prices. Using historical data, we can regress the holding period returns for flour (R_{fl}) against the holding period returns for the futures contract (R_f), denoting the coefficient of the change in the price of the futures contract for flour by β_{fl}:

$$R_s = \alpha + \beta_{fl} \, R_f + \varepsilon$$

We can also regress the change in the price of bread against the change in the price of the futures contract, denoting the coefficient of the futures contract in this regression as β_b:

$$R_s = \alpha + \beta_b R_f + \varepsilon$$

These results produce an estimated hedge ratio of

$$\text{Hedge ratio} = \beta_b - \beta_{fl}.$$

If β_b is 0.92 and β_{fl} is 0.62, the estimated hedge is 0.30. In other words, for every unit of bread that the bakery produces, a futures contract covering only 0.30 units of flour is needed. Issues in estimating these hedge ratios arise concerning the appropriate interval over which to measure price changes (daily, weekly, and monthly), nonsynchoneity in the various price series, and possible day-of-the-week, time-of-the-year biases.

3.4.2. The theoretical approach

There are many instances in which it is also possible to determine a hedge ratio using a theoretical model. One of the most common examples is the use of duration by financial institutions in constructing hedges. Recall that duration is the time-weighted maturity of an asset. Financial institutions hold a portfolio of long and short positions in financial assets, many of which have a promised cash flow stream that is known in advance. Efforts by financial institutions to match, at least to some extent, the duration of their assets and liabilities is called **gap management**. Some financial institutions attempt to match the duration of their assets and liabilities exactly so that they are immunized from risk due to fluctuations in interest rates. Others may have objectives such as limiting potential losses due to interest rate fluctuations to a stated amount.

Financial institutions can use both securities and derivatives to accomplish their hedging goals. Spot and futures prices converge at maturity so that it might well make sense to hedge a portfolio of bonds using futures contracts covering a portfolio of underlying assets with similar maturities.

3.5. Summary of Section 3

A natural long position can be hedged by shorting a futures contract, writing a call, or buying a put. A natural short position can be hedged by going long a futures contract, buying a call, or writing a put. Futures contracts are used in hedging two-sided natural positions. Options are used to hedge both one-sided and two-sided natural positions. If the natural position is two-sided, the futures position offsets both gains and losses on the natural position. A hedger may prefer to buy an option, risking the loss of the premium in exchange for the possibility of gain on the underlying asset. The hedger may also prefer to write an option, risking the possibility of loss on the underlying asset in exchange for the possibility of gaining the option premium. In this case the protection afforded by the hedge is limited to the amount of the option premium. Hence, the amount of protection provided by writing a call or put depends on whether and to what extent the option is in the money and the amount of the excess premium. By writing options, the hedger also potentially sacrifices at least a portion of the potential gain from the underlying asset.

4. Additional hedging topics

4.1. Hedge funds

In 1949 Alfred Windslow Jones developed the concept of the **hedge fund,** which had three unusual characteristics, namely, the use of leverage, short selling, and performance fees.[1] Jones's goal was to emphasize asset selection ability rather than market timing. In an extreme case the monetary amount of assets held long and short would be equal and the short position would be chosen to hedge the systematic risk of the long positions. If the hedge is successful the portfolio has exposure only to the unsystematic risk of the long securities. Of course, if the fund manager can also select assets likely to experience unfavorable unsystematic events, the fund could benefit from superior asset selection in the short positions as well. Because the combined long and short positions are presumably less risky, the fund manager can increase the risk level of the fund through the use of leverage. The third innovation is the use of a performance fee in which the fund manager receives, say, 20% of the profits of the fund rather than a fee based on the amount of assets the fund hold.

---

[1] See Lederman, Jess and Robert A. Klein, eds. 1995, Hedge Funds. Chicago: Irwin or a description of hedge funds.

An example might help. Suppose that a fund started with 100 USD. The fund might borrow another 40 USD and buy stocks with an aggregate value of 140 USD. To offset part of the risk the fund might short stocks with an aggregate value of 60 USD so that if the hedge is effective the net exposure to the systematic risk of the market is 140 − 60 = 80 USD or 80% of the initial value of the portfolio. The fund pays interest on 40 USD of borrowing but earns interest on the proceeds of the short sale, although at a lower rate.

Jones's fund was highly successful, but obscure, until the publication of an article by Carol Loomis (1966).[1] This article publicized Jones's outstanding results. Over the previous ten years the Dreyfus fund had the best performance among mutual funds. Jones's results bested Dreyfus's performance by 87 percentage points even after taking fees into account. The publication of this article began a period of rapid growth of the hedge fund industry. In early 2011 assets in the hedge fund industry were estimated to be about 1.9 trillion USD.[2]

4.2. Value at Risk

The Group of Thirty's Global Derivatives Study Group made twenty recommendations for derivatives dealers and end-users and four recommendations for regulators and governments.[3] From our perspective the most important recommendations were:

- "Dealers should mark their derivatives positions to market, on at least a daily basis, for risk management purposes."
- "Dealers should use a consistent measure to calculate daily the market risk of their derivatives positions and compare it to market risk limits."
  - o "Market risk is best measured as 'value at risk' using probability analysis based upon a common confidence interval (e.g., two standard deviations) and time horizon (e.g., one-day exposure)."

---

[1] Loomis, Carol J., 1966, The Jones nobody keeps up with, Fortune, April, 237-247.

[2] From Wikipedia citing Daily FT , 24 January 2011.

[3] Global Derivatives Study Group (1993). The Group of Ten's web address is:http://www.group30.org/.

o "Components of market risk that should be considered across the term structure include: absolute price or rate change (delta); convexity (gamma), volatility (vega) time decay (theta); basis or correlation; and discount rate (rho)."

- "Dealers should regularly perform simulations to determine how their portfolios would perform under stress conditions."

Value at risk is the monetary amount of the decline in value that a derivatives portfolio can be expected to sustain during a specified percentage of time periods.[1] The specified percentage is typically either 1% or 5% and the time period can be daily, weekly, monthly or any other period. Daily periods are commonly used. Assume a 3% probability and a daily time period. If value at risk is 100,000 USD then this portfolio can expect to sustain a decline in value of 100,000 USD or more on three days out of 100 days. This number can be presented to the board of directors, investors, and regulators to indicate the exposure of the firm.

There are a number of ways to calculate value at risk (for a more detailed discussion see Linsmeier and Pearson (1996)). We will describe a popular method used to calculate daily value at risk. Assume that we are calculating daily value at risk using a 5% probability. The first step is to identify the variables that determine the value of each derivative in the portfolio. For interest rate derivatives this might involve exchange rates for each currency and interest rates for each currency. Typically interest rates for multiple points along the yield curve are required. Other types of derivatives might require stock and commodity prices, inflation rates and the like. Once these factors are identified data is collected for the last 101 days. Then beginning at day −100 the percentage change in each variable is calculated for each day to yield 100 changes. For each variable the oldest change is applied to yesterday's value to create a hypothetical value for today. Then the next oldest change is applied to the first hypothetical value to create a hypothetical value for tomorrow. This process continues until 100 projected values are calculated for each variable.

---

[1] J.P. Morgan developed a popular value at risk program called RiskMetrics®. Morgan has announced that it is spinning off its risk metrics group. The J.P. Morgan web address is: http://www.jpmorgan.com/.

In the next step the projected values for each day are used to value each derivative and an aggregate portfolio value is obtained for each day. These portfolio values are sorted from highest to lowest and the portfolio value with the fifth largest loss is the value at risk.

The value at risk measure has a number of obvious limitations. If too much historical data is used the measure may not reflect current market conditions. If too little data is used the measure may not be accurately estimated. Moreover, the measure will not indicate what would happen to the portfolio if the determinants of the derivatives' values took on a worst case or very extreme outcome. These might be more important than more common but less drastic outcomes. This is undoubtedly the reason that the Group of Thirty recommends **stress testing** of the portfolio. This allows for the consideration of more extreme outcome than are likely to be found using the value at risk approach.

4.3. Hedging foreign exchange risk

Firms are increasingly operating globally. Hence, they may have revenues and expenses in many different currencies. Companies have developed sophisticated strategies for managing their foreign exchange and minimizing risk due to currency fluctuations. Companies such as Coca-Cola use hedging to protect their profits (see Box 4-2). There has also been a marked increase in cross-border portfolio investment in recent years. This trend has lead to interest in whether investors should hedge their foreign exchange exposure. The answer for individuals and portfolio managers may not be the same as the answer for companies. We have argued that risk is inherent in investments. Some argue that currency risk should be fully hedged all of the time, some that currency risk should be partially hedged, and some that there is no need for hedging. The question is whether hedging risk due to currency fluctuations reduces risk sufficiently to justify its cost. There has been no definitive answer to this question, but a number of factors that are useful in making a decision have been identified.

Fully hedging currency risk. In our discussion of futures we indicated that the net hedging hypothesis argued that speculators must be compensated for taking risk from hedgers. Using similar reasoning, Perold and Schulman (1988) conclude that "to assume one will receive a premium

---

Box 4-2. Coca-Cola tells analysts that currency hedging protects profits

According to its president, M. Douglas Ivester, of Coca-Cola uses hedges mostly to protect itself from currency fluctuations. The firm benefits from a portfolio effect because of its dealings in almost 200 currencies. Firms dealing in fewer currencies would not realize this portfolio effect to the same extent. The purpose of Coke's hedging program is to eliminate risk to earnings due to currency fluctuations, according to Ivester. To increase this protection Coke extended its hedging horizon, which had been three months, to three years.

For additional details see: Wall Street Journal, May 7, 1996.

---

for holding foreign currency is to assume the other side of the transaction will pay a premium for U.S. dollars, that 'they need our currency more than we need theirs.'" While there may be periods of time when one can earn a premium for holding a particular currency, there is no reason to believe that these premiums will be consistently positive or negative. Moreover, these authors present evidence that there is substantial risk reduction from hedging currency risk.

Partial hedging. Black (1990) develops a model that leads to the proposition that there is an optimal hedge ratio that applies to every investor who holds non-domestic securities. "When average risk tolerance is the same across countries, every investor will hold the same mix ... of exchange risk ((in a diversified basket of foreign currencies)."

No hedging. According to Delaney (1997), "many investment experts don't believe in hedging to begin with. They argue that it's nearly impossible to predict currency swings, the ascents and declines cancel each other out over the long term anyway, and hedging mechanisms are just an added expense for shareholders." Froot (1993) argues that the benefits from currency hedging are short-term and that over the long term the costs of hedging outweigh the benefits. According to Mark Riepe, a vice president of Ibbotson Associates,[1] "Those who choose to hedge their foreign

---

[1] Ibbotson provides consulting services and data. The firm's web address is http://corporate.morningstar.com/ib/asp/detail.aspx?xmlfile=1409.xml

currency raise the correlation with U.S. stock, and so the diversification benefit won't be nearly as great (Clements 1997)."

Additional factors are also related to whether a portfolio should be hedged:

Concentration of investments in a particular country. An international portfolio manager may like the prospects for the companies in a particular country. These companies may come from different industries and provide diversification benefits. In the process of making decisions about which companies to buy an international portfolio manager is also making decision about the currency exposure of the portfolio. While the underlying investments may be desirable, the concentration of currency exposure in particular countries may not. In this case the fund managers may seek to hedge this currency exposure.

Diversification benefits from holding a portfolio of currencies. It is well established in financial economics that there are risk-reduction benefits from holding a diversified portfolio. The view that an international investor who buys a portfolio of international stocks should hedges all on the currency risk so that only the domestic currency is held is contrary to this prescription. Hedging typically concentrates the portfolio in a single currency. In some cases this would be beneficial, but in many cases it would be harmful. Suppose that a Russian investor held an internationally diversified portfolio, but, in an effort to reduce currency risk, hedged 100% back into the Russian rubble. When the rubble lost the majority of its value vis-à-vis other currencies in the late 1990s, the investor would be significantly worse off. In late 1997 the value of the Indonesian rupia decline from just over 2,000 to one USD at mid year to more than 15,000 to one USD less than six months later. Indonesians who hedged their international holdings back into their domestic currency certainly suffered significant losses.

If it is agreed that a portfolio's currency exposure should be hedged, then who should do the hedging? Traditional equity and fixed income managers may not be equipped to manage currencies. There is a growing practice of employing a **currency overlay manager** to actively and independently manage foreign exchange exposure. The overlay manager begins with the existing exposure of the portfolio and attempts to reduce risk through the net sale of non-domestic currencies. Note that the overlay manager is hedging as defined in this chapter. The goal is to reduce risk. Hence, Layard-Liesching (1997) argues that "the currency overlay manager is not permitted to increase preexisting currency exposure by the net purchase of foreign currency." Manning (1996) reports on the status of currency overlay management in a number of countries. The largest overlay market is in the US. Outside the U.S. the largest markets are in the Netherlands and Australia. Though the potential markets in Japan and the UK are large, the market for overlay management has been slower to develop than in the U.S. where the currency overlay management business grew from almost nothing at the beginning of the 1990s to have more than 40 billion USD under management by the mid 1990s.

Some investment professionals view currencies as a separate asset class that should be managed in the same way as any other assets. Arnott and Pham (1993) argue that currency markets are not efficient because two of the largest participants do not have a profit motive. Central banks attempt to limit exchange rate volatility and corporations seek to hedge their inventory positions and cash flows. Levich and Thomas (1993) take a similar view stating that "A more aggressive active currency overlay strategy earned the highest returns ... of any strategy we examined, yet was less risky than not hedging at all." According to Day (1997) "active management of currencies ... can enhance portfolio returns" (p. 39).

5. Summary

Hedging is the acquisition of positions to reduce or eliminate risk of loss due to price fluctuations. To the extent that an individual or firm is pursuing another goal, they are not hedging. A perfect hedge completely eliminates risk due to fluctuations in the price of the hedged asset. Producers, financial institutions, individuals and others often face risk from fluctuations in the price of assets owned or contracted for. Natural longs face risk of loss due to price decreases in an asset and natural shorts face risk due to price increases in an asset. Two-sided natural longs and shorts face a loss from a price move in one direction, but reap a gain from a price move in the opposite direction. One-sided natural longs and shorts face a loss from a price move in one direction, but do not gain from a price move in the opposite direction. Natural longs require short hedges and natural shorts require long hedges.

Hedging fulfills the economic function of allowing the transfer of risk due to price fluctuations. Speculators take positions in derivative contract with the intention of profiting from price changes. Since it is unlikely that the desired positions of long and short hedgers would exactly match, speculators are necessary for the functioning of hedging markets. But hedging and speculation are clearly different activities.

One approach to determining the needed hedge position is to compare the economic outcome from having financial exposure to the underlying asset with the economic outcome from the contemplated hedging position. If gains on the hedge offset losses on the underlying asset, the proposed hedge is effective. Assessing the hedge in this way is the economic outcome approach. Alternately, the substitute action approach identifies hedge positions by examining whether a purchase or sale of the cash asset would eliminate risk due to fluctuation in the asset's price. Then, a substitute action involving, say, the purchase or sale of a futures contract, is undertaken instead.

There are a number of reasons that a futures position might not provide a perfect hedge including basis risk, changes in the relationship between the cash price of an asset and its futures price, maturity mismatch, contract size mismatch, and the use of cross-hedges by hedging one asset using a derivative on another asset.

Historically, many firms, especially financial institutions, have hedged using securities, but derivative instruments have become increasingly popular for hedging. These derivative instruments include long and short positions in futures and forward contracts, and the purchase and writing of puts and calls. For two-sided natural positions, common hedging strategies are long and short futures positions, and the purchase of puts and calls. Hedgers purchasing options give up the premium paid in return for the protection afforded by the option. On the other hand, hedging using options may preserve potential for gain from price movements in the underlying asset if the natural position is two-sided. Hedgers who use futures typically give up the potential for gains if the price movement in the underlying asset is favorable in return for the protection afforded when the price movement in the underlying asset is unfavorable. Hedging with futures avoids the necessity of paying the option premium. It is also possible to hedge by writing options, but these hedging strategies generally provide less protection from unfavorable price movements in the underlying asset. On the other hand, depending on the actual movements in the price of the underlying asset, the financial outcome may be superior to the other alternatives.

The concept of the hedge fund was developed by Alfred Windslow Jones. A hedge fund uses leverage, short selling, and performance fees. Short selling is used to create portfolios in which short positions hedge long positions, reducing the exposure of the portfolio to market forces. Leverage is used to increase the risk level of the fund and performance fees compensate managers for favorable performance. There has been rapid growth of the assets being managed by hedge funds.

The Group of Thirty recommended that firms holding portfolios of derivatives calculate the risk of the portfolio on a daily basis. The risk measure commonly used is called value at risk and measures the monetary amount of the decline in value that a derivatives portfolio can be expected to sustain during a specified percentage of time periods. A statement that the daily value at risk is 42,300 USD at the 5% probability level means that this derivatives portfolio can be expected to sustain a loss of 42,300 USD or more on 5 of the next 100 days.

Questions

1. Define hedging.
2. Do hedging programs contribute to a firm's profitability?
3. Why are both hedgers and speculators needed in a market?
4. Define natural long and natural short and give examples of each.
5. Define two-sided and one-sided hedges and give examples of each.
6. Describe hedging by pension plans using real assets.
7. Define the economic approach to hedge determination and the substitute action approach.
8. List five potential problems in obtaining a perfect hedge using futures?

References

Arnott, Robert D., and Tan K. Pham, 1993, Tactical currency allocation, Financial Analyst Journal 49, 47-52.

Black, Fischer, 1990, Equilibrium exchange rate hedging, Journal of Finance 45, 899-907.

Clements, Jonathan, 1997, International investing raises questions on allocation, diversification, hedging, Wall Street Journal, July 29, p. C1.

Day, Paul, 1997, Active currency management to enhance returns, in Managing Currency Risk. Charlottesville, VA: Association for Investment Management and Research, 39-49.

Delaney, Kevin J., 1997, Funds generally don't hedge Asian bets, Wall Street Journal (December 22), p. C27.

Froot, Kenneth A., 1993, Currency hedging over long horizons, working paper no. 4355. Washington, D.C.: National Bureau of Economic Research.

Global Derivatives Study Group, 1993, Derivatives: Practices and Principles. Washington, D.C.: Group of Thirty.

Layard-Liesching, Ronald, 1997, The role of currency overlay managers, in Managing Currency Risk. Charlottesville, VA: Association for Investment Management and Research, 50-57.

Levich, Richard M. and Lee R. Thomas, 1993, The merits of active currency risk management: evidence from international bond portfolios, Financial Analysts Journal 49, 63-70.

Linsmeier, Thomas J. and Neil D. Pearson, 1996, Risk measurement: an introduction to value at risk. Working paper, Urbana-Champaign, IL: University of Illinois.

http://wueconb.wustl.edu:8089/eps/fin/papers/9609/9609004.html

Manning, Mike, 1996, Currency risk management—recent developments, emfa (European Derivative Investment and Funds Association) Newsletter (September) 14-16.

Perold, Andre F., and Evan C. Schulman, 1988, The free lunch in currency hedging: implications for investment policy and performance standards, Financial Analysts Journal (May/June), 45-50.